Brodie's Notes

G000146049

List continued overleaf

List continued from previous page

Harper Lee	**To Kill a Mockingbird**
Laurie Lee	**Cider with Rosie**
Christopher Marlowe	**Dr Faustus**
Arthur Miller	**The Crucible**
Arthur Miller	**Death of a Salesman**
John Milton	**Paradise Lost, Books I and II**
Robert C. O'Brien	**Z for Zachariah**
Sean O'Casey	**Juno and the Paycock**
George Orwell	**Animal Farm**
George Orwell	**1984**
J. B. Priestley	**An Inspector Calls**
William Shakespeare	**Antony and Cleopatra**
William Shakespeare	**As You Like It**
William Shakespeare	**Hamlet**
William Shakespeare	**Henry IV Part I**
William Shakespeare	**Henry IV Part II**
William Shakespeare	**Julius Caesar**
William Shakespeare	**King Lear**
William Shakespeare	**Macbeth**
William Shakespeare	**Measure for Measure**
William Shakespeare	**The Merchant of Venice**
William Shakespeare	**A Midsummer Night's Dream**
William Shakespeare	**Much Ado about Nothing**
William Shakespeare	**Othello**
William Shakespeare	**Richard II**
William Shakespeare	**Romeo and Juliet**
William Shakespeare	**The Tempest**
William Shakespeare	**Twelfth Night**
George Bernard Shaw	**Arms and the Man**
George Bernard Shaw	**Pygmalion**
Alan Sillitoe	**Selected Fiction**
John Steinbeck	**Of Mice and Men** and **The Pearl**
Jonathan Swift	**Gulliver's Travels**
J. M. Synge	**The Playboy of the Western World**
Dylan Thomas	**Under Milk Wood**
Alice Walker	**The Color Purple**
Virginia Woolf	**To the Lighthouse**
W. B. Yeats	**Selected Poetry**

ENGLISH COURSEWORK BOOKS

Terri Apter	**Women and Society**
Kevin Dowling	**Drama and Poetry**
Philip Gooden	**Conflict**
Margaret K. Gray	**Modern Drama**
Graham Handley	**Modern Poetry**
Graham Handley	**Prose**
R. J. Sims	**The Short Story**

General editor: Graham Handley MA Ph.D.

Brodie's Notes on L. P. Hartley's

The Go-Between

G. E. Brown

First published 1978 by Pan Books Ltd

This revised edition published 1993 by
THE MACMILLAN PRESS LTD
Houndmills, Basingstoke, Hampshire RG21 2XS
and London
Companies and representatives
throughout the world

ISBN-10: 0-333-58125-3 paperback

ISBN-13: 978-0-333-58125-4 paperback

Printed and bound in Great Britain by

Antony Rowe Ltd, Chippenham and Eastbourne

Contents

Preface

The intention throughout this study aid is to stimulate and guide, to encourage your involvement in the book, and to develop informed responses and a sure understanding of the main details.

Brodie's Notes provide a clear outline of the play or novel's plot, followed by act, scene, or chapter summaries and/or commentaries. These are designed to emphasize the most important literary and factual details. Poems, stories or non-fiction texts combine brief summary with critical commentary on individual aspects or common features of the genre being examined. Textual notes define what is difficult or obscure and emphasize literary qualities. Revision questions are set at appropriate points to test your ability to appreciate the prescribed book and to write accurately and relevantly about it.

In addition, each of these Notes includes a critical appreciation of the author's art. This covers such major elements as characterization, style, structure, setting and themes. Poems are examined technically – rhyme, rhythm, for instance. In fact, any important aspect of the prescribed work will be evaluated. The aim is to send you back to the text you are studying.

Each study aid concludes with a series of general questions which require a detailed knowledge of the book: some of these questions may invite comparison with other books, some will be suitable for coursework exercises, and some could be adapted to work you are doing on another book or books. Each study aid has been adapted to meet the needs of the current examination requirements. They provide a basic, individual and imaginative response to the work being studied, and it is hoped that they will stimulate you to acquire disciplined reading habits and critical fluency.

Graham Handley 1990

A close reading of the set book is the student's primary task. These Notes will help to increase your understanding and appreciation of the book, and to stimulate *your own* thinking about it: *they are in no way intended as a substitute* for a thorough knowledge of the book.

Page references in these Notes are to the Penguin edition of *The Go-Between*, but references are usually given to particular chapters, so that the Notes may be used with any edition of the novel.

The author and his work

Leslie Poles Hartley was born at Whittlesey in Cambridgeshire on 30 December 1895, and died on 13 December 1972, aged 76. He was recognized as one of the most distinguished English novelists of the twentieth century. In 1948 he was awarded the Black Memorial Prize, followed by the Heinemann Award in 1954, and he gave the Clark Lectures at Trinity College, Cambridge, in 1964. In 1956 he was awarded the C.B.E., and early in 1972 the Royal Society of Literature made him a Companion of Literature, an honour which is restricted to ten living British writers. In addition to these public honours Hartley had the satisfaction of always having his work received with respect by reviewers, particularly after the publication of *The Shrimp and the Anemone* in 1944; and the majority of his novels have remained in print and enjoyed steady sales. Towards the end of his life, Hartley's work was given a further boost when film companies took an interest in his novels. In 1971 Joseph Losey directed a distinguished film version of *The Go-Between* with a script by Harold Pinter; and a film of *The Hireling*, directed by Alan Bridges, was in production at the time of Hartley's death. Late in 1977 Hartley's work was given even wider circulation when BBC 2 showed three television films adapted by Alan Seymour from the *Eustace and Hilda* trilogy.

Hartley was born into the middle-class world in which most of his fiction is set. His father was an extremely successful Peterborough solicitor who made a great deal of money, largely because he retired early and became the owner of a brickworks. L. P. Hartley was later to make use of this aspect of his background in his novel *The Brickfield* (1964). The family consisted of two sisters and Leslie, and during their childhood much time was spent at Hunstanton, the 'Anchorstone' in which *The Shrimp and the Anemone* is set. Leslie was educated at Harrow and Balliol College, Oxford, and served during the First World War as a second lieutenant in the Norfolk Regiment, from which he was invalided out with a bad heart.

Many of these circumstances and experiences later found their way, in transmuted form, into his fiction.

Hartley received his degree at Oxford in 1922. At the university he had been co-editor of the *Oxford Outlook*, and he decided to pursue his interest in literature on a professional basis when he came down from Oxford. At first he made his mark as a reviewer for magazines such as the *Spectator*, and the *Saturday Review*, and in fact he continued to review regularly until the 1950s, often, as his obituary in *The Times* states, 'writing his notices from Venice, where he lived for part of each year until the Second World War.' Venice is the background for Hartley's first short novel, *Simonetta Perkins*, a work of less than a hundred pages which was published in 1925 following the issue of his first volume of short stories, *Night Fears*, in 1924.

Although he was not pressed financially, as he had a private income, Hartley continued to review professionally throughout the years prior to the Second World War. After *Simonetta Perkins* he brought out only one more volume of short stories, *The Killing Bottle* (1932), before the publication in 1944 of *The Shrimp and the Anemone* – the first novel in his *Eustace and Hilda* sequence. Peter Bien records that Hartley had begun to write *The Shrimp and the Anemone* in the early 1920s 'and had at least half finished it by the mid thirties. At this point, however, he abandoned it because he feared it might be considered more autobiographical than it really was.' But, thanks to the encouragement of several of his friends who knew of its existence, Hartley finally completed the book; it was his first full-length novel.

He followed it in rapid succession with the remaining volumes of the trilogy in 1946 and 1947, having published the brief *Hilda's Letter* in 1945. The trilogy established Hartley as a leading novelist and he continued to publish novels at regular intervals until his death. *The Boat* (1950) was followed by the extremely successful *The Go-Between* in 1953. The flow of novels was interrupted by two more volumes of short stories, in 1954 and 1961; and he published his *Collected Short Stories* in 1968. In addition Hartley brought out, in 1969, a collection of his literary criticism which included his Clark Lectures on the America novelist Nathaniel Hawthorne. His last novel, *The Will and the Way*, was published posthumously in 1973.

In spite of the fact that he lived through a period in which writers such as James Joyce and Virginia Woolf were experimenting with new techniques in writing novels, L. P. Hartley was one of a group of writers whose technical approach would have been recognized by the great Victorian novelists, even though their subject matter was often of a nature that the Victorians would have felt themselves debarred from dealing with. Rubin Rabinovitz, in *The Reaction Against Experiment in the English Novel, 1950–1960*, puts the case well when he writes that one of the chief arguments persuading writers to work in the mainstream tradition 'was that the experimental novelists, particularly Joyce in *Finnegans Wake* and Virginia Woolf in *The Waves*, had baffled ordinary readers to such an extent that they had stopped reading novels altogether.' No doubt Hartley's rejection of new forms can be seen as a conscious reaction against the experimentalists, which reflected his wish to find a means of effective communication with a wide readership. But it should also not be overlooked that he saw himself as a direct descendant of a line of traditional novelists that can be traced back to Samuel-Richardson. As David Holloway wrote in his appreciation of Hartley in *The Daily Telegraph* on the day after his death, 'Henry James and Jane Austen were his great influences, and his name could be mentioned in their company without dishonour.'

This is not to say that Hartley is always an uncomplicated writer. Indeed, the richness of his writing frequently centres on his conscious use of symbolism to make his effects in an indirect way. Many readers react well to this technique, but it is only fair to record that he has sometimes been criticized for it. C. P. Snow, for example, wrote in 1958, 'With the only two senior living English novelists of distinction who have as it were, underlined their symbols, E. M. Forster and L. P. Hartley, one is – or at least I am – more comfortable elsewhere in their books.' The reader must make up his own mind on this question.

I mentioned earlier that most of Hartley's work is set in the middle-class world into which he was born. Frederick R. Karl writes that 'His world of upper middle-class gentility unfolds without fuss ...' To a certain extent this is true. 'Yet though his world is a small one, and apparently demure, the smallness and the demureness are deceptive, for his world can uncannily reflect the violence and the conflicts from which it is seemingly isolated,' said Walter Allen in his *Tradition and Dream*. The 'violence and the conflicts' to which Walter Allen refers cannot be ignored, and often in Hartley's fiction we are aware of his critical attitude towards the hypocrisies of the world of the upper middle class.

Several of the novels set in the early years of the twentieth century contain characters whose natural development is blighted by the rigidities of the class structure or by sexual ignorance and inhibition. Nevertheless, in spite of his awareness of the limitations inherent in the English social structure of the early twentieth century, Hartley always appears to hark back nostalgically to a time when the social fabric gave an impression of permanence. It is as though he wishes to criticize the middle-class world but not destroy it. This attitude was responsible for the one really surprising novel that Hartley wrote – *Facial Justice*, which, according to Bernard Bergonzi, was started in 1953, though it was not published until 1960. The book has been described by one critic as 'a kind of religious science-fiction, part fantasy about the future and part satirical fable about the standardization and neutralization of men and women.' Bergonzi states that the book 'stems from a distaste for the ideology and cultural atmosphere of post-war British socialism' (*The Situation of the Novel*, 1970). Certainly it was an unexpected book for Hartley to write, in that it is set in the future 'at some point after a Third World War'. His other novels, when they have not dealt with contemporary affairs, have been set in the past. On this occasion, however, the urgency of his feelings drove Hartley outside his usual field as a novelist. The book is not really experimental in technique, but it is a worthy addition to the list of anti-utopian novels written in the twentieth century by writers such as Jack London, Yevgeny Zamyatin, Aldous Huxley and George Orwell.

It is too soon after Hartley's death to say with certainty

whether his books will last, though David Holloway wrote of the *Eustace and Hilda* trilogy that, 'This novel sequence will no doubt become an English classic.' Holloway put his finger on Hartley's strength when he wrote that 'he knew a great deal about human relationships of many different kinds, and within the limits that he set himself he wrote about them with a skill that at moments touched on genius.' This does not seem to be too large a claim, and it is reinforced by the writer of Hartley's obituary in *The Times* who, after drawing attention to the way in which 'the apparent narrowness of his rendering of life was more than compensated for by its depth', went on to suggest that Hartley was at his best in the *Eustace and Hilda* volumes and *The Go-Between*: 'works which, it is impossible not to think, will be read for many years to come'.

Setting and background

The greater part of the novel is set in 1900, with the framework of the Prologue and Epilogue set in 1952. Apart from those sections dealing with Leo's schooldays and Chapter 1 in which Hartley convincingly sketches in the background to the life lived by Leo and his mother in a village near Salisbury, the events of those parts of the book set in 1900 take place in Norfolk. To narrow down the location still further: the 1900 action takes place mainly in the house and grounds of Brandham Hall, 22 km (nearly 14 miles) from Norwich. Exceptions are: the trip Leo makes with Marian to buy clothes in Norwich (Chapter 4); Leo's excursions to Black Farm on the occasions when he sees Ted Burgess (Chapters 7, 9, 10 and 15); the picnic (Chapter 8); the cricket match and the supper that follows it in the village hall (Chapters 11–13); and the scene in which Leo says good-bye to Ted by the sluice (Chapter 19).

By placing the main events of the novel in 1900 and limiting the action to the immediate vicinity of Brandham Hall, Hartley is able to portray a privileged way of life that was shortly to disappear for ever, and concentrate on a limited number of characters interacting in an enclosed situation.

Many of the comments on Hartley's treatment of class distinctions (see *Themes*) should be read in conjunction with this present section. Here, however, attention is drawn to Hartley's careful choice of period and the way in which this underpins both his treatment of themes and the use of symbolism that is so basic to his method of writing.

For the purposes of this novel the date *had* to be 1900. As Peter Bien has pointed out, 'Hartley deliberately tried to evoke a golden age, that of the turn of the century (with the Boer War included as just a hint of what was to come).' In case the pointers to the decline of Britain's overseas influence and power implied by the references to the Boer War and reinforced by the wounds received in South Africa by Lord Trimingham are not enough, Hartley allows Marian to mention the deaths of Denys and Marcus in the Great War casually in her conversation with Leo in the Epilogue (pp.276–7). The leisured life of the middle classes was coming to an end, and in retrospect the Boer War seems to have been a forewarning of changes to come.

In many minor ways the accuracy of Hartley's evocation of setting is impressive. He portrays a world in which the middle classes sent their children away to school as a matter of course, a time when to enter domestic service was a logical thing to do for large numbers of young men and women, who expected to end their working lives in the employment of the same family. There was security, as well as stagnation and exploitation, in the system. Hartley recreates a world in which transport is by train or by horse-drawn vehicle, and roads are dusty in the summer, as they have not yet been covered with tarmac. In his Brandham Hall there is no telephone, and people have to communicate by letter – which accounts for the way in which Ted and Marian involve Leo in their love affair, as a messenger.

Hartley has taken immense care over detail in *The Go-Between*. His allusions to contemporary events are always accurate. 1900 *was* one of the hottest summers on record, and, as has been pointed out in the textual notes, it is very appropriate that he should make Denys mention the cricketer, R. E. Foster, in Chapter 11 (p.129). His references to aspects of the Boer War, such as the date when Lord Roberts entered Pretoria, are all carefully researched and fit exactly into the time scheme of the novel. The result is to make the reader think that if Leo is so meticulous in his recall of all these occurrences he must be trusted as narrator of the other momentous events of that summer at Brandham Hall. The honesty with which he sets down his memories combines with the shift of focus in the Prologue and Epilogue to produce a feeling of verisimilitude that is artistically satisfying to the reader.

I have referred earlier to the physical limitation of setting in *The Go-Between*. This again adds to the book's impact. Hartley is able to examine closely a small number of characters, and to show us how they affect one another. He concentrates his attention on the inhabitants of the hall and their visitors (in particular, Leo and Lord Trimingham), and sets Ted Burgess apart from the others both socially and in terms of location. The novel's structure requires Leo to be involved in the three-sided affair of Marian, Ted and Trimingham; and consequently he has to be brought into the action as bearer of the messages and letters between Ted and Marian. It is therefore essential for the plot that Ted should live quite near to the hall, but just far enough away to make communication with Marian difficult. In addition, we should not overlook the important fact that Ted's land – and it is only rented from Trimingham – is separated from that of the Maudsleys by a river, emphasizing that Ted is an 'outsider' figure. This point is reinforced when he has to meet Marian in the decaying outhouses behind the hall, as he would not have been considered an acceptable suitor for her.

It should be noted that while Hartley is very specific about setting the main events of the novel in Norfolk, he does not stress the individuality of the background as strongly as he does in, for example, *The Shrimp and the Anemone*. The scene in which Leo visits Norwich Cathedral (Chapter 4) is firmly located, but Hartley does not make a central point of the impact the building has on Leo, as he does when Eustace Cherrington visits Frontisham in the earlier novel and is overpowered by the west window of the church.

It is fair to state that for the purposes of his plot in *The Go-Between* Hartley could have set the novel in any agricultural county at the turn of the century, provided that it contained a hall with a nearby village and river, and provided that it was sufficiently far away from Leo's home to emphasize the fact that he was on strange ground and could not return to his mother's house at a moment's notice. (The interested reader, however, may be tempted by the fact that the film of *The Go-Between* was shot on location at Melton Hall in the village of Melton Constable, Norfolk. If he is prepared to brave the 'No Entry' signs prominently displayed on the lodge gates and go up the long drive, he will be faced by a sight very similar to that of the south-west prospect of Brandham Hall.)

Chapter summaries, critical commentary, textual notes and revision questions

Epigraph (facing p.7)

The stanza is taken from a poem of fifty-three lines written in July 1837 by Emily Brontë (1818–48), best known for her novel, *Wuthering Heights* (1848). The lines are appropriately chosen to precede *The Go-Between*: the boy Leo is metaphorically long dead, a 'child of dust'; in the summer of 1900 he experienced 'The bright blue sky', and was 'conducted' towards the 'bower' (a place closed in with foliage) in Chapter 23 (p.262) when he and Mrs Maudsley came upon Marian and Ted making love in the outhouse near the spot where the deadly nightshade had grown.

Prologue

The Prologue is set in 1952. The narrator (later revealed as Leo Colston) discovers a diary for 1900 when he is sorting through his papers. He is reluctant to open the diary, which he recalls contains a record of events that have prevented him from fulfilling himself in later life. Nevertheless he does open it, to find the date 1900 surrounded by the signs of the zodiac. He remembers the attraction these signs once held for him and his feeling that the new century would herald a Golden Age. Glancing through the entries Leo recalls how he was bullied at school because of his pretentious use of the word 'vanquished' in his diary, which his schoolmates then defaced. In an attempt to regain face, he formulated two curses incorporating the names of his chief tormentors, and wrote them in a nonsense code in blood in the diary, which he deliberately left where it would be discovered. Almost immediately he was set upon again by the bullies, and that night he shed tears in bed. Next day Leo learned that his two enemies had fallen from the school roof during the night. The other boys believed that his curses had caused the accident, and he acquired the reputation of a magician. Reading further in the diary, the adult Leo comes upon references to a holiday spent at Brandham Hall in July. Leo realizes that the clue to his subsequent development lies in the diary entries and the memories which they are capable of arousing – if he can only bear to face them. He decides to do so.

The narrator immediately grasps the reader's attention with the finely balanced first sentence. Then he mentions the diary which is to reveal so many painful memories to him. Tension is built up by the narrator's reluctance to open it. Notice how Hartley makes use of the details, such as the drab, flowerless room and the cold rain beating on the windows to emphasize the adult Leo's dispirited state and loneliness. When he begins to read what he had written in 1900, Leo mentions the 'catastrophe', thus pointing forward to the tragic outcome of events at Brandham Hall. The symbolic associations of the signs of the zodiac with the characters of the novel will be developed more fully later. Leo's interest in magic, as illustrated by the curse he puts on Jenkins and Strode, anticipates the spell he draws up at Brandham Hall to break the spell he believes Ted has cast on Marian. Hartley stresses the inescapable links between the older Leo and his schoolboy self by the imaginary dialogue between the two towards the end of the prologue. The section ends on a note of anticipation, with Leo determining to face up to the memories of half a century ago.

Eton collars Broad stiff white collars separate from shirts and worn prominently outside jackets. Part of the uniform of boys at private schools at the turn of the century. (Term derived from Eton College, the famous public school near Windsor, founded in 1440.)

sea-urchins Round marine animals, frequently covered with spikes.

negatives Rolls of exposed film from which prints can be made.

combination lock ... rows of letters Padlock that can only be opened by arranging letters in a particular sequence chosen by the person who locks the mechanism.

the children of the past i.e. the various past selves of the narrator, revealed to him by the objects in the collar-box.

Of all the exhibits Calls to mind a court of law. The narrator, by re-examining the events of 1900, is in a sense, putting himself on trial.

zodiac Zone or belt of the heavens traversed by the sun in the course of a year. Ancient astronomers divided the zone into twelve equal parts and allotted to each a sign of the zodiac.

the Lion epitomized ... had it in us to be The narrator's name is revealed to be Leo, later in the chapter (p.21). Hartley has chosen it ironically since the events described in the book deprive Leo of any possibility of developing 'imperious manhood'. He may also have had in mind the decline of England as a great power in the twentieth century, as the lion is the symbol of England.

She was dressed adequately ... her long hair This description is recalled in Chapter 4 (pp.57–8) where the parallel between the Virgin and Marian is made explicit.

a Golden Age In Greek and Roman mythology the Golden Age was the first and best age of the world, during which man was idyllically happy.

who probably had few facial types ... command i.e. who could only draw a limited number of kinds of face.

Hercules Mythological hero who possessed immense strength.

as to the Water-carrier ... a farm-labourer Points forward to the link between Ted Burgess, a tenant farmer, and the Water-carrier. He is associated with water (a symbol of life) in Chapter 4 (pp.53–5) and is described by Leo as the Water-carrier in Chapter 23 (p.262).

Sagittarius – Aquarius The Archer and the Water-carrier (Latin).

3 breaks ... riping Leo's diary entries reflect his youth: he misspells 'brakes' and 'ripping'. A 'brake' was a horse-drawn wagonette; 'ripping' was schoolboy slang for excellent, splendid.

preparatory school School for children (usually boys) where pupils are prepared for entrance to higher schools, especially public schools.

Harrow Famous public school in Greater London, founded in 1572. Traditional sporting rival of Eton.

pros and cons Arguments for and against a course of action.

to swank To show off (slang).

intoxicated by my almost sensuous ... coming to me Ironic in view of what happens later.

poetic justice Ideal justice.

from a gun they had so thoroughly spiked i.e. from something they believed they had discredited beyond redemption. The metaphor is taken from the practice of rendering an enemy's cannon unusable by driving a metal spike into the touch-hole where the firing charge was ignited.

Sanskrit Ancient language of the Hindu sacred writings.

Peau de Chagrin Novel by Honoré de Balzac (1799–1850), translated into English as *The Wild Ass's Skin*.

I had shot my bolt I had done all I could.

funk Coward (slang).

dorm Abbreviation of dormitory.

I was keeping a weather eye open for i.e. I was on the lookout for.

the San Abbreviation of sanatorium.

ragging Playing rough jokes upon, tormenting, physically attacking (slang).

curses that had literally ... Jenkins and Strode The two boys had fallen from the school roof.

Tuesday 10th. 84.7 degrees In his diary Leo records the temperature for each day according to the Fahrenheit scale.

I did not have to turn ... would be blank Throughout the Prologue Hartley builds up our curiosity as to what happened in the narrator's past. Sentences such as this whet our appetite to know more.

like the loosening phlegm ... to come up Carefully chosen image which forewarns the reader that what is to be revealed will be unpleasant.

my interment policy i.e. the narrator has buried the unpleasant memories of 1900 until the present (1952, as he reveals at the end of the paragraph).

You flew too near to the sun ... scorched Recalls the myth of Icarus, the son of Daedalus, who tried to escape from imprisonment in Crete by means of wings made by his father. Icarus flew too close to the sun, the wax attaching his wings was melted, and he fell into the Aegean Sea and drowned.

fallen angels Angelic beings who were damned. The characters from Leo's past are compared to the angels led by Satan who revolted against God and were expelled from Heaven and forced to live in Hell.

Thanet Former island, which now forms the North East portion of Kent.

for many years ... only a written word Implies that the events of 1900 caused the narrator to guard himself against close relationships. Nobody has called him by his Christian name for a long time.

Chapter 1

The events of Chapters 1 to 23 inclusive are set in 1900. This chapter deals with Leo's circumstances, and with events leading to his visit to the Maudsley family at Brandham Hall in

July. Leo lives alone with his widowed mother in a village near Salisbury. During the summer term he is happy at school because the other pupils respect his reputation as a magician. They persuade him to use his powers to obtain a day's holiday for the school, and are rewarded when an epidemic of measles causes those boys who are unaffected to be sent home. At the beginning of July, Mrs Maudsley, the mother of one of Leo's dormitory companions, writes to ask his mother to allow him to spend the month in Norfolk. The invitation largely results from the fact that the Maudsleys have been impressed by Leo's address – Court Place, West Hatch – though in reality it is not a large house. Mrs Colston hesitates over accepting the invitation on Leo's behalf, but it is arranged that he should travel to Brandham Hall on Monday, 9 July. Leo tells his mother that he will not need summer clothes as he knows it will not be hot. Partly from motives of economy she agrees to pack only thick clothes for him. As the date for the visit approaches Leo wants to back out, but his mother insists that he should go.

Hartley packs a lot into this chapter, all the necessary details being given before the action of the novel proper gets under way. We are made aware quite distinctly of the class differences of the time (note the reason for Mrs Maudsley's invitation). We are also made aware of Leo's deprivation in the loss of his father and what we might call the reserved possessiveness of his mother. Notice how Hartley captures Leo's reluctance to go, as well as the unusual qualities of the loner. Leo obviously believes in his own forecasting ability and, as so often, his confidence is misplaced, for the heat is to be exceptional.

Salisbury County town of Wiltshire.
as witness the fact ... to me later It does later in the chapter (p.29).
crocodile Line of children walking in pairs.
a jobbing gardener One who hires himself out for as long as he is needed; not attached to a single employer.
crank Eccentric person.
indeed, I owe to them ... cares of life i.e. the money raised from the sale of the books was invested by Leo to produce a private income.

landau Four-wheeled horse-drawn carriage with a movable top.

livery stable Stable from which horses and carriages could be hired.

savoir-faire Quickness to see and do the right thing (French).

I had hopes of the cricket season This prepares the reader for Leo's success on the cricket field in Chapter 12 (pp.137–40).

bowdlerize To censor. The word commemorates Dr Bowdler (1754–1825) who produced an edition of Shakespeare's works in 1818 minus words and expressions he believed would cause embarrassment and offence when read aloud in a family.

They were very much subdued, and so was I Another pointer to the way in which the events of the summer affected Leo.

a whole holiday A full day's holiday.

the vessels of salvation i.e. the trunk and the tuck-box.

J.C. Mr Cross, the Headmaster.

aperitif Alcoholic drink taken before a meal to stimulate the appetite.

I had relaxed ... invulnerable Ironic, in view of later events.

heat was my enemy ... I dreaded it A forewarning of the unfortunate way events will turn out for Leo during the heatwave at Brandham Hall.

the Clerk of the Weather Imaginary official humorously supposed to control the state of the weather.

the Season Period of the summer when members of fashionable society assembled in London.

Town London.

Promise me you'll let me know ... she said Yet when Leo does so, his mother writes to say that it would be a mistake to leave Brandham Hall sooner than originally planned (Chapter 20, pp.218–20) . If she had cooperated in allowing him to go home he would have been spared the horrifying revelation of Ted and Marian in the outhouse (Chapter 23, p.262), together with the knowledge of Mrs Maudsley's breakdown and Ted's suicide.

You needn't do anything *violent*, need you No, but indirectly Leo's actions as 'postman' lead to the violence of Ted's death.

bloomer Blunder (slang).

Chapter 2

The adult Leo is reminded by his diary of certain facts about the visit to Brandham Hall. He learns from it that he was met at Norwich station by Marcus Maudsley and driven 22 km (13¾ miles) to the Hall. In the diary he reads a description of the Hall, copied by him as a boy from a directory of Norfolk. He recalls the room he shared with Marcus, and brief conversations with his host and hostess. He remembers that there were a lot of young people staying at the Hall, and that it took him a few days to realize that two of them were Denys and Marian Maudsley. He had not been impressed by the weak Denys, but recalls coming upon the seated Marian when she thought she was alone, and examining her closely, as Marcus had told him that she was very beautiful. Other diary entries concern the horses and equipment kept in the stables, but Leo's adult memory is stirred by a reference to having seen a deadly nightshade plant when he was exploring, alone, some derelict outhouses. The chapter ends with a description of the plant. Young Leo decides not to mention its presence to Mrs Maudsley, in case she has it destroyed. It fascinates him and he wants to visit it again.

A number of the forecasting elements of this chapter are given in the summary above. Of major interest is the 'looking back' technique – the flashback so common in films – and the exactitude of the diary. By giving us the factual base, Hartley prepares us for the excursion into the memory which gives the novel a graphic intensity – as if the events were happening in the present and not in the past. Again there is a sharp focus on class awareness, difference, period behaviour. But the real concentration, in all its atmospheric and symbolic density, is on the plant which is at the centre of Leo's mind, at the centre of the novel's structure, and which reaches out with deadly associations into this fictional world.

the eve of that fateful Friday Another pointer towards traumatic events later in the book.

Pepys's Samuel Pepys (1633–1703), Secretary of the Admiralty, kept a diary from 1660 to 1669. The editors of the Bell edition wrote in 1970 that 'he used a method (mixing shorthand with heavily-abbreviated longhand, and occasionally adding scrambled shorthand and full longhand) which presents many difficulties in transcription and publication.' Although Pepys's diary remained untranscribed for more than a century after his death it cannot really be described as being in code.

'break' Solve or read back coded material.

Norwich County town of Norfolk.

We drove 13¾ miles ... disappeared again Leo's childishness is shown by his insistence on the absolute accuracy of distances, and by his mis-spelling of sight.

Gainsborough and Reynolds Thomas Gainsborough (1727–88) and Sir Joshua Reynolds (1723–92) were prominent English painters, particularly famous for their portraits.

Cuyp, Ruysdael, Hobbema Aelbert Cuyp (1620–91), Jacob van Ruysdael (1628?–82) and Meindert Hobbema (1638–1709) were Dutch painters known chiefly for their landscapes.

Teniers the Younger David Teniers the Younger (1610–90) was a Flemish artist. His paintings in the smoking-room at Brandham Hall 'are not shown' to the public because of their erotic quality. See Chapter 18, p.205.

has the gift of the livings of i.e. has the right to appoint clergymen to the benefices of.

Threadneedle Street Street in London's commercial centre in which the Bank of England is situated. Mention of Mr Maudsley's business address reinforces the point that the mercantile classes were in the process of ousting the aristocracy at the time in which the novel is set. This is most effectively symbolized by Hartley's device of having Trimingham, a member of the Winlove family, stay at Brandham Hall as a guest in his own house.

when the ladies retired It was customary at the time (and still is in some circles) for the ladies to withdraw at the end of dinner, leaving the gentlemen to their port, brandy and cigars.

She always seemed to take up ... and he less This sentence brilliantly sums up the relative forcefulness of Mr and Mrs Maudsley.

but when I see her in dreams ... face at all Points forward to the novel's terrible climax. See Chapter 23, p.262.

Ingres or Goya Jean Auguste Dominique Ingres (1781–1867), a French painter; Francisco José Goya y Lucientes (1746–1826), a Spanish artist known especially for his portraits.

Her glance most often rested ... daughter Establishes the close link that exists between mother and daughter, but also hints at the fact that Mrs Maudsley feels the need to keep a close watch over Marian.

Hottentot Member of native race of Southern Africa.

hourglass figures Figures resembling an hourglass in shape because of the fashion that demanded an extremely small waist.

He would grow warm He would become very animated.

Atropa belladonna Belladonna means 'beautiful lady'. See the section on *Symbolism*.

for did not my mother's botany book say so Reinforces the impression of Leo's childishness and literal-mindedness.

Chapter 3

The day after Leo's arrival at Brandham Hall sees the beginning of a heat wave, and Marcus and Leo check the temperature on a thermometer kept near the house by Mr Maudsley. That night Leo tries a spell to bring the temperature down: nothing happens. Guests begin to comment on the way he appears to be suffering in the heat, and when Mrs Maudsley asks him whether he left his summer clothes at home he tells her that his mother must have forgotten to pack them, and then bursts into tears. Marian offers to take Leo into Norwich on the following day, a Friday, to buy him some summer clothing, saying that it can be for his birthday. Mrs Maudsley obviously disapproves of Marian's suggestion and tries to make her wait until the following week when another guest, Trimingham, who is due to arrive on Saturday, will be able to accompany her. But to Leo's delight Marian persists, and it is arranged that the visit to Norwich shall take place as originally suggested. Members of the family offer to pay for particular items of clothing for Leo. The chapter ends with Marian's checking his wardrobe. She admires the way in which his clothes have been mended (perhaps realizing that his mother is responsible), and tells him that she knows the summer clothes (which he told Mrs Maudsley his mother had forgotten to pack) are an invention.

A chapter of embarrassment for Leo – the heat and his unsuitable clothes, with the class difference ironically pointed up by Hartley. But it is a chapter of opportunism for Marian – the idea of the trip to Norwich is obviously her way of shaping her own romantic involvement. Again the sequence is packed with information, but there is a degree of tension generated between Mrs Maudsley and Marian. Part of the period authenticity is established by the boys' slang, and we feel for Leo in his outsiderness – and his consciousness of his own comparative poverty. Already Marian is making inroads into his immature heart, the major aspect of her ability to use Leo for her own ends.

game-larder Small building in which dead game was hung until it was ready to eat.

No, but my mother ... obliquely Another indication that Mrs Maudsley is a stronger personality than her husband.

Norfolk jacket Loose-fitting single-breasted jacket with pleats at the front and back.

sport my cricket togs i.e. wear my cricket clothes (slang).

cads People guilty of failure to behave like gentlemen (slang).

the Black Arts Magic.

au fond At bottom, basically. (French)

glass Mirror, looking-glass.

fifteen shillings ... halfpenny Approximately 78 new pence.

Goodwood Fashionable race meeting held every July at Goodwood, near Chichester in Sussex.

was stealing my thunder Was pushing me out of the limelight, taking the attention away from me.

like two steel threads ... each other Excellent simile used to emphasize the opposing wills of Marian and her mother. Mrs Maudsley wants her daughter to marry Hugh Trimingham (see also Chapter 4, p.52), and would prefer her to postpone the Norwich visit until he can accompany her. Marian has mixed motives for wishing to go on the Friday; she genuinely wants to buy new clothes for Leo, but she also plans to meet Ted Burgess without anyone knowing.

Of course, unless your father ... horses In this and her three succeeding speeches Mrs Maudsley shows her irritation with Marian by hopefully implying that her husband may want the horses, by suggesting that Marian sometimes shops unwisely, by contradicting Denys and by questioning whether Leo's new clothes should include ties.

I'll stand him a tie I'll buy him a tie (slang).

Bags I the bags I make first claim on (slang) the trousers (slang).

Chapter 4

Leo enjoys his visit to Norwich with Marian on the Friday. They have lunch in a hotel after a morning spent buying clothes for him. Marian leaves Leo for an hour after lunch telling him to visit the Cathedral, and when he goes to meet her he sees her in the distance saying good-bye to a man. Back at Brandham Hall Leo shows his new clothes to the assembled company, and his green suit causes particular comment. Marian tells her mother that they saw nobody they knew in Norwich. Next day a bathing party is arranged and Leo accompanies the others; but Mrs Maudsley will not let him bathe until he has received his mother's permission. On the walk to the river Marcus tells Leo that Trimingham is due to arrive that evening, adding that he has suffered facial injuries in the war and that Mrs Maudsley wants Marian to marry him. When they reach the bathing-place the group find someone swimming there. Denys makes himself agreeable when he discovers that it is Ted Burgess, a tenant farmer. While Leo is watching the swimmers Ted leaves the water. 'Leo observes him secretly and is impressed by his powerful physique. Marian is heard complaining that her hair is wet, and Ted dresses quickly and goes. On the way back to the hall Leo protects Marian's dress by letting her arrange her hair on his dry bathing suit fastened round her neck. He is delighted to be able to serve her in this way and Marian appears strangely elated.

The reader, like Leo, is intrigued by the meeting with the man, though the buying of the clothes is so important to him, raising his status in his own eyes and endearing Marian to him. Marian of course tells the reflex lie when they get back to Brandham. The green clothes are emphatic of Leo's greenness – his innocence and inexperience. The swimming party underlines once more the class divisions: the appearance of Ted Burgess underlines his physicality, the sexuality to which Marian is – secretly – responding. The contrast with the scarred Trimingham is still to come. There is real pathos in Leo's service to Marian – a kind of innocent sensuality through the contact of her hair with his bathing suit.

O altitudo Literally a reference to the height of the Cathedral spire; metaphorically indicative of Leo's exhilarated mood, caused by his love for Marian.

Sir Thomas Browne Sir Thomas Browne (1605–82) was a physician who spent most of his life in Norwich. He is chiefly famous as the author of *Religio Medici* (1643).

She seemed to be saying good-bye ... hat Yet Marian tells her mother that they did not see anyone in Norwich (p.49). See also Epilogue, p.266.

Marian said yes ... another name on it Another indication that Marian tells lies easily, and this is a pointer to the later lies about visiting Nannie Robson (e.g. Chapter 23, p.253).

Lincoln Green In former times bright green cloth was made at Lincoln and was worn by hunters in Sherwood Forest.

Robin Hood Legendary medieval outlaw associated with
Sherwood Forest. He was believed to rob the rich to aid the poor.

Maid Marian Legendary companion of Robin Hood. Leo is
thinking of Marian Maudsley when he imagines himself acting
as Robin Hood.

caught like a moth ... intensity never varied Brings out the
strength of Mrs Maudsley's personality, and prepares the reader
for the way in which she dominates Leo in Chapter 23 (e.g.
pp.253–6, and pp.261–2).

Hard cheese Bad luck (slang).

pro-Boer Supporter of the Boers (South African farmers of
Dutch origin) in the second of two wars fought against them by
Great Britain in 1899–1902.

The Soldiers of the Queen ... Leave You Popular patriotic
songs of the day.

relief of Ladysmith Ladysmith, a town in Natal, was besieged
by the Boers from 2 November 1899 to 28 February 1900, when
it was relieved, after three unsuccessful attempts, by Sir Redvers
Buller. There was great rejoicing in Great Britain when the
news was received.

not even a Mr It is not until Chapter 6, p.71, that Leo realizes
that Trimingham is a viscount. See for example, pp.61–2.

He can't go quite as he is i.e. because he is practically naked.

bathing machine Wheeled changing-hut that could be pushed
out into the water.

He doesn't swim badly ... farmer Most of Denys's speeches in
this section are very condescending.

What can they do ... conscious of themselves Leo has already
noted Ted's powerful body 'which spoke to me of something I
did not know' (p.56). He later receives a shocking visual answer
to his present question (Chapter 23, p.262).

She was in a strange, exalted mood ... source Marian is
excited by the thought of Ted Burgess, which makes her
physically very aware of herself; whereas Leo is attracted
towards Marian, without her realizing it.

Chapter 5

The chapter begins with a description of family prayers at
Brandham Hall. On Sunday morning Marcus feels unwell
and stays in bed; he asks Leo to give his regards to Trimingham. Leo finds himself sitting beside Trimingham at prayers,
and is struck by the sight of his scarred face. After breakfast
Leo tells Mrs Maudsley that Marcus is ill. When he goes up to

their room Marcus informs him that he may have measles. Leo takes his prayer-book and goes downstairs to await the group's departure for church; on the walk to church Leo talks to Marian, and Trimingham overtakes them.

Marcus's illness provides Leo with more freedom in the time to come, and he is thus able (though he doesn't yet know it), to play the role of the 'go-between'. In a sense, Leo's awareness of Trimingham's scarred face inadvertently mirrors Marian's repulsion. Notice how Leo is now fitting much more easily into the social set-up at Brandham.

Fast i.e. free and easy in the moral sense.

looking red-eyed As a result of crying.

But supposing she didn't want to marry him This shows Leo's precocious insight into emotional possibilities, and prepares the reader for later events.

his good side i.e. the side that is not disfigured.

Janus God in Roman mythology whose function was to guard doorways and gates, and the state in time of war (which makes the parallel with Trimingham doubly effective.) Janus was always painted or carved with two faces – one on the front of the head and the other on the back.

Beauty and the Beast Characters in a fairy-tale in which Beauty saves her father's life by agreeing to live with the Beast. Beauty's love frees the Beast from a spell which has been cast on him, and he becomes a handsome prince before marrying her. Parallels between this story and *The Go-Between* are very slight.

de rigueur Required by etiquette (French).

Cripes Expression of astonishment. Slang for 'Christ'.

ruddy Mild form of 'bloody'.

jolly old kirk i.e. church. As Leo says, 'when any excitement ... was afoot, we often lapsed into schoolboy talk, even away from school' (p.64).

egg Person (slang).

And have you got any old button ... collection Marcus continues to act in a sophisticated fashion even when ill. Here he reminds Leo to take a coin for the collection, but jokingly implies that he could put a button in the plate.

smelling-bottle Bottle containing smelling salts.

Ta-ta ... shammer Leo does not think that Marcus is shamming but it would go against their schoolboy code to show too much concern about his health.

les convenances Conventional proprieties (French).

shilling Coin worth five new pence.

Revision questions on Prologue–Chapter 5

1 Describe, as fully as possible, the older Leo's reactions on discovering the diary for 1900.

2 Give a detailed account of Leo's changing responses to Mrs Maudsley's invitation to stay at Brandham Hall.

3 What is the first impression Leo receives of Marian?

4 Why does Hartley make Leo say that his spiritual transformation took place in Norwich?

5 Describe Leo's reactions to the presence of (a) Ted and (b) Marian in the bathing scene in Chapter 4.

Chapter 6

In church Leo realizes – on examining the mural tablets, each commemorating a Viscount Trimingham – that the ninth Viscount may still be alive. He concludes that the Maudsleys and their guests at Brandham Hall can justifiably bask in the reflected Trimingham glory. Bringing his mind back to the service, Leo reacts against the term 'miserable sinners', believing that a person should face life's problems by using his own resources. Walking back from church Leo is joined by Trimingham, who introduces himself. After a while Leo realizes that Trimingham is the ninth Viscount and feels foolish at being so slow on the uptake. He reveals his Adoration of Marian to Trimingham, who asks him to tell her that she left her prayer-book in church and that he has it. At first Marian cannot understand the message because of Leo's mispronunciation of 'Hugh', the ninth Viscount's christian name. She does not go to retrieve her prayer-book, and Trimingham appears disappointed. When they reach the hall they find that the doctor has come to visit Marcus. After luncheon Mrs Maudsley tells Leo that he has been moved into another bedroom in case Marcus has anything infectious. Leo changes into his green suit and leaves the house, looking for adventure.

Leo's education continues, his eager and enquiring mind stimulated by the examination of the tablets in church and by his conversation with Trimingham. The class awareness to which I have constantly referred in these commentaries is emphasized by Leo's actually talking to a real viscount: once again his innocence – his failure to grasp things despite his cleverness – is evident. Trimingham employs Leo as a go-between for the first time over Marian's prayer-book. The mispronunciation of 'Hugh' is both comic and pathetic, but the chapter ends on an exciting note: Leo, without Marcus, is free to make his own adventures.

those fortunate periods when history ... without dates Leo is putting forward a schoolboy's opinion here. A few lines later he writes of 'things to be learnt, to be forgotten, to be examined about, perhaps to be punished for forgetting' (p.68).

Life was meant to test a man ... tested Ironic in view of the disastrous results on Leo of his stay at Brandham Hall.

Perhaps if you ... begging letter Note Trimingham's dry humour throughout this conversation. A begging letter is one sent to a rich person, usually by someone unknown to him, requesting financial assistance.

I blushed at the hit Trimingham is gently mocking Leo in view of the earlier misunderstanding about his own title (p.71).

spifflicating. A.1. Colloquial terms for 'excellent', 'first-rate'.

I could run errands for her ... messages Ironic in view of later events.

dog-cart Two-wheeled cart with cross-seats arranged back-to-back; drawn by horses, not dogs.

You mustn't call him Mister ... surgeon Surgeons are called 'Mr' to differentiate them from physicians, who are given the courtesy title of 'doctor'.

Doctors always come at lunch-time ... rules Humorous suggestion by Trimingham implying that doctors hope to be invited to stay for lunch.

Chapter 7

Outside, the temperature is eighty-four degrees, and Leo revels in the heat, which seems to have liberated everything including himself. He reflects on all that Brandham Hall represents and feels that he has left everyday life behind in coming here. He wants to be alone and decides to walk along the path leading to the bathing-place. He crosses the sluice and soon finds himself outside a farmyard, which he enters. He climbs a straw-stack down which he then slides, cutting his knee in the process. The farmer sees him and threatens him for trespassing. Leo recognizes him as Ted Burgess and tells him that they met at the bathing-place. Ted's manner changes when he realizes that Leo is from the Hall, and he dresses his cut knee. Leo asks if he can do anything for Ted in exchange for his kindness, and is told that he can take a message for him. After showing Leo the horses Ted asks if he can trust him and whether Leo can give Marian a letter from him in secret. He tells him that it concerns business and that he is to destroy it if he cannot get her on her own. Leo leaves with the letter, and arrives back at the hall at teatime. He tells everyone how kind Ted has been, and Marian takes him to the bathroom to dress his knee. Leo gives her the letter from Ted, and this puts her into some confusion. She tells him that he must not tell anyone about the letter, as it would get everyone into trouble.

What appears to be a schoolboy exploit – the coming upon the farmyard – is fraught with consequencs. Notice that Ted adjusts his attitude towards Leo when he realizes that he is staying at Brandham. Like Marian, Ted is an opportunist. The go-between is now operating in earnest, trapped by the lovers without any recognition of what is going on. Leo is essentially 'decent': he wants to do the right thing in gratitude for Ted's kindness, but we feel his vulnerability both at the farm and when he returns to Brandham and Marian tends his knee. The narrative tension is raised, for secrecy implies the chance of discovery, and the plot now hinges on this situation.

the others, the companions of the Zodiac i.e. the adults
staying at Brandham Hall.
There was no one about This one-line paragraph containing
four monosyllables heightens the suspense here.
holler Emit a loud cry.
gentleman farmer Country gentleman who farms, but is not
dependent on farming for his main source of income.
You're a Spartan i.e. you are brave. (The inhabitants of Sparta
in ancient Greece were famous for their powers of endurance.)
He always seemed to speak ... body One of many examples of
Hartley's emphasis on Ted's physicality. See also Chapter 4,
pp.54–7, Chapter 7, pp.83 and 87, and Chapter 15, p.170.
Wild Oats, he answered ... grin Ted grins because to sow

one's wild oats means to indulge in youthful excesses before settling down. The phrase is appropriate to his own reputation as 'a bit of a lady-killer' (Chapter 18, p.204).

topping Excellent (slang).

the place where you pull the chain i.e. the lavatory.

on the square Honest, trustworthy.

détente Relaxation (French).

peaked Sickly.

She almost snatched ... gracious, so I have The effect of Ted on Marian is shown here and on the previous page where she seems not to have heard his name mentioned, yet immediately leads Leo to the bathroom, partly to hear more about him. Here she eagerly 'snatches' the letter, and is so agitated that she forgets about having already bandaged Leo's knee.

Chapter 8

Mrs Maudsley betrays her anxiety to please Lord Triming-ham when she announces her plans for excursions and picnics. On one expedition Trimingham calls Leo 'Mercury', after the messenger of the gods, and this fires his imagination. He dozes off after the meal and wakes to hear Marian (who thinks he is still asleep) suggesting that he should be left out of future excursions as he must be bored. Leo is quite pleased at the prospect of being able to explore things on his own. When they get back to the hall he finds a letter from his mother, and writes to her before visiting the game-larder to check the temperature. It has reached ninety-four degrees that day, and he hopes that a hundred degrees will be recorded soon. After speaking to Mr Maudsley, Leo wants to be on his own, but Trimingham asks him to find Marian to play croquet. He meets her on the track leading to the outhouses and she agrees to join Trimingham. When Leo tells her that he may go to slide down Ted's stack next day Marian asks him to take a letter for her and claims not to know Ted very well. She then tells Leo that she has decided against playing croquet, but he succeeds in persuading her to join the others.

A significant chapter in the movement of the plot. There is a terrible irony in Leo being called Mercury, and we suspect that Marian is again being opportunistic when she suggests allowing more freedom from adult involvement for Leo. Notice how letters play an important part in the structure of the narrative. The three-way pull – Trimingham, Ted, Marian – is now being exerted upon Leo, with the invitation via him from Trimingham to Marian for croquet. Games too are important pivots (you will note the importance of the cricket match later) though the real game is one of duplicity and, soon, moral blackmail of Leo.

he's your little lamb Allusion to the nursery rhyme beginning 'Mary had a little lamb', in which the lamb follows Mary everywhere she goes.

he makes us thirteen Some people believe it is unlucky to have thirteen in a group, particularly at a dinner table. Note the unconscious irony of Mrs Maudsley's remark. If Leo had not been at Brandham Hall to carry messages between Ted and Marian perhaps their affair would not have developed and the tragic conclusion would have been avoided. In a sense Leo brings bad luck to Mrs Maudsley, though Marian's affair with Ted had started before his arrival.

Roman tortoise The parasols clustered together to keep out the sun remind Leo of Roman foot soldiers advancing in close formation under a protective roof made by holding their shields above their heads.

is a bit of a lad i.e. is one for the ladies.

bearing-reins Fixed reins from bit to saddle, which force horses to arch their necks.

c/o i.e. care of.

out of touch Unable to do something well or easily.

ha-ha Sunken fence or ditch separating lawn from park.

dead ground Artillery term. Hidden ground lying below the level of visible land.

have her in your pocket i.e. have control over her.

along the cinder track ... walking rather quickly Marian has been to see Ted, and is hurrying away from their meeting-place.

Because you like T – Mr Burgess A slip of the tongue almost gives away how well Marian knows Ted.

Chapter 9

On three occasions in the week before the cricket match, Leo carries messages between Ted and Marian. He speculates on the contents of the letters, but cannot arrive at a satisfactory answer. Meanwhile the very hot weather continues. When Marcus is allowed to get up on the Friday Leo believes that this will make it impossible for him to carry any more messages for Ted and Marian. But she slips him a note which she does not have time to seal, and he sets off for the farm, leaving Marcus at the Hall. Leo wants to know what the letter contains, but will not remove it from its envelope. However, when he reads the words which are visible under the open flap it is obvious to him that Marian and Ted are in love.

With the picking up of the pace through Leo's fuller employment, there is of course an increase in tension as Leo ponders a situation which he cannot possibly grasp, given his upbringing and the general innocence of his nature. His awakening is therefore all the more rude and sudden, and allied to this are his own guilt feelings at what he has read. His own innocent love for Marian emphasizes the torture that he suffers. We feel, too, that with Marcus's recovery he, Leo, will be able to get out of his commitment.

I walked beside it ... four farm-labourers So that the men cannot see when Leo passes the letter to Ted.

rush-baskets In which the farm workers have brought their food and drink.

a sheaf the reaper ... smear of blood See section on *Symbolism* for comment on the language used here.

after breakfast orderly-room Military language used humorously, but further emphasizing Mrs Maudsley's formidable qualities.

pull the wool over ... eyes Deceive, hoodwink.

Lord Roberts Lord Roberts of Kandahar (1832–1914) was British commander-in-chief against the Boers in South Africa from 1899 to 1900.

Kitchener Lord Kitchener of Khartoum (1850–1916) was British commander-in-chief in the Boer War from 1900 to 1902.

Kruger Paulus Kruger (1825–1904); an Afrikaner soldier and statesman who was president of the Transvaal republic from 1883 to 1899.

de Wet Christian Rudolf de Wet (1854–1922); a Boer general during the wars with Britain.

Dr Livingstone and Stanley David Livingstone (1813–73) was a Scottish medical missionary and explorer who discovered Victoria Falls. Henry Morton Stanley (1841–1904), a British explorer and journalist, was sent to Africa by the *New York Herald* in 1871 to find Livingstone, who had not been heard of for a long time. Leo humorously mentions that his exchanges

with Marcus were 'much more expansive' than those of Stanley and Livingstone since, after his lengthy search, Stanley is reported to have confined himself to saying, 'Dr Livingstone, I presume.'
spooning Behaving amorously, i.e. hugging and kissing.
Pax Peace! Truce! (slang).
the Eleventh Commandment Jokingly supposed to be 'Thou shalt not be found out.'
cribbing Copying another schoolboy's work.

Chapter 10

Leo feels let down by his discovery, but goes to the farm to deliver the letter. He tells Ted that because of Marcus's recovery he will be unable to continue to act as postman, but Ted brings pressure to bear on him by saying how much the letters mean to Marian. Ted informs Leo that one of the mares is going to have a foal, and answers some of his questions about 'spooning' in a general way. Finally he makes a bargain with Leo: he will tell him all about 'spooning' if he will continue to deliver the messages and letters.

In fact he uses the excuse almost as soon as he meets Ted, a pathetic indication of the way he has been hurt by Marian's few words. He has reckoned without Ted's capacity for moral blackmail (I am not suggesting that this is entirely without sympathy for the boy), and the focus on what Marian will feel further undermines Leo. But the deep pathos here is on the 'spooning' sequence, with Leo's anxiety to know (and fully understand) brilliantly captured by Hartley. I suggest that there is immediate emotional involvement here for the reader, since for many of us our own transition from sexual ignorance to later understanding may not have been easy. In other words, we feel for and with Leo.

Not Adam and Eve ... apple See Genesis, 3.
sell Colloquial term for deception, disappointment.
'front' Main promenade of seaside resort.
chap-fallen Dejected, downcast.
His ruddy face went mottled ... breath Here Ted is forced to think of the possible consequences of his affair with Marian. Although he hurriedly dismisses the idea we learn later that Marian did become pregnant. See Epilogue, p.269.
to make assurance doubly sure See *Macbeth*, IV, 1, 83.

Revision questions on Chapters 6–10

1 How does Hartley make use of humour in his description of Leo's first meeting with Trimingham?

2 Write a brief account of the scene in which Marian dresses Leo's knee and his gives her the letter from Ted.

3 In what ways does the recovery of Marcus complicate life for Leo?

4 Describe Leo's state of mind when he realizes that the messages he has been carrying between Ted and Marian are love letters.

5 What impression does Hartley give of Ted in his conversation with Leo about 'spooning' in Chapter 10?

Chapter 11

On Saturday the sky is cloudy and the temperature is slightly lower than it has been. At breakfast the conversation is about the cricket match which is to take place that day. Denys is worried that Ted Burgess's hitting will prove a problem for the Hall team. Leo is selected to be twelfth man, and is asked by Trimingham to find out if Marian will sing 'Home, Sweet Home' at the concert that evening. Her answer is obviously intended to hurt Trimingham, but Leo persuades him that she meant it as a joke. After a buffet luncheon the members of the team walk to the ground, where Leo talks briefly with Ted Burgess. The Hall team bats first and loses five wickets for fifty-six runs, Trimingham scoring only eleven. Mr Maudsley bats soundly, but Denys is run out when he foolishly refuses a short single once too often. Mr Maudsley gets his fifty and the Hall total is 142. The village innings starts at five o'clock, with two hours left for play.

The cricket match symbolizes the battle between Ted and Leo for Marian and has the fine irony of Leo's catch, itself a symbol of their being caught out later. Note the change in the weather, betokening other changes which will later be evident. Trimingham's request for 'Home, Sweet Home' is a coded message to Marian of how he sees her at the centre of his life (their coming shared home together), and Leo is now adapting his role by altering emphases when he wants to – here his telling Trimingham (to save him being hurt) that Marian's reply was jocular. This first part of the match is speckled with significance – Trimingham's comparative failure, Mr Maudsley's determined resistance, the class struggle between villagers and their rich patrons, all this is finely conveyed. To end the chapter between innings is a masterly dramatic stroke on the part of Hartley. Who will win – Hall or Village, Trimingham or Ted?

before he's set i.e. before he has begun to play with confidence.

I shall put myself on i.e. I shall act as bowler myself.

Duck Batsman's score of nought.

A. N. Other Fabricated name and initials included in a list of players in a cricket match when the final composition of the team is not yet known. (Name = another.)

twelfth man First reserve player in a cricket team. The twelfth man may field in place of an injured player, but he may not bat or bowl.

You're the one ray of light Marian presumably means because he carries her messages to Ted, but Leo does not take it that way.

it was obvious that he couldn't Because of his wounded face. See Chapter 5, p.61.

putting on side i.e. adopting superior airs (slang).

as if a battle were in prospect Very appropriate. See section on *Symbolism*.

you should make him run errands ... Burgess Trimingham does not suspect that this already happens.

the farmer's white flannels The appearance of the village players is 'nondescript' (p.127), but Ted is appropriately dressed for the game. By drawing attention to this, Hartley emphasizes that Ted is a worthy opponent for Trimingham.

scoring-cards Cards on which to record players' scores, details of their dismissal etc. More usually known as score-cards, as on p.135.

white sheets Used as sight-screens behind the bowlers at each end of the ground.

R. E. Foster Reginald Erskine Foster (1878–1914) played cricket for Oxford University, Worcestershire and England. In 1900 he scored 171 for Oxford v. Cambridge and ten days later made a century in each innings (102 not out and 136) in the Gentlemen v. Players match. It is appropriate that Hartley has Denys refer to the outstanding amateur batsman of the season.

he asked for middle and leg i.e. he asks the umpire to tell him when his bat is directly covering the two stumps nearest to him.

Father Time Personification of time as an old man with scythe and hourglass. Hartley may have had in mind that there is a weather-vane representing Father Time on top of the grandstand at Lord's cricket ground in London; but it was not there in 1900.

the position of the field i.e. where the fielders are standing.

loose balls Badly directed balls from the bowlers.

a boundary Hit worth four or six runs.

swingers Balls that are hard to hit because they deviate in the air after leaving the bowler.

when the signal ... raised against him Apt metaphor.

he was run out i.e. he failed to reach the popping crease (line at the other end of the pitch).

It wasn't cricket Colloquial expression meaning that something infringed accepted codes of behaviour.

It was an ascendancy of brain ... suspicious Hartley's irony is evident here.

having just made his fifty Traditionally, batsmen scoring fifty or a hundred are applauded by spectators, and usually by the opposing team.

the game was replayed ... times i.e. its outstanding features were animatedly discussed.

Chapter 12

The early village batsmen are out cheaply and the match looks like being 'a walk-over'. When Ted Burgess is nearly bowled first ball Leo realizes that he wants him to do well. Ted is an unscientific hitter, but he soon reaches his fifty. Leo notices that Marian is flushed with excitement. When one of Ted's hits injures a fielder Leo is called on to field as substitute. Trimingham is determined to get Ted out, and with less than ten runs required for victory puts himself on to bowl. He quickly takes a wicket and with only one wicket to fall bowls to Ted, who hits a glorious four. Three more runs will win the match and Leo desperately wants Ted to make them. Next ball, however, Leo makes a brilliant catch to dismiss him and win the game. He is possessed by conflicting emotions and feels compelled to apologize to Ted for getting him out, but Ted praises his catch. The ladies from the Hall show interest as Ted returns to the pavilion, but Leo notices that Marian does not look up.

Certainly the question asked at the end of the commentary on Chapter 11 is resolved here – or is it? Leo's sympathies are early called out on behalf of Ted, whose innings represents his physical potency, the mark of his conquest of Marian. The irony of Leo's catch has been mentioned earlier. It represents Leo's role in the ultimate revelations of the plot – he brings down the lovers unwittingly, and changes their future history, just as here he changes the course of the game. This is evidence of Hartley's careful structuring. Equally good are his shifts of focus from the field to the watchers and from Trimingham to Ted to Leo. Cricket is a man's world, but we are aware throughout that Marian is the prize sought.

walk-over Easy victory.

skittling out ... side i.e. dismissing their batsmen in rapid succession.

skier Ball hit high into the air.

looking like victors ... stricken field Fine simile. The recumbent fielders resemble the dead and dying on a battlefield.

to see the red light i.e. to be aware of the danger.

pull it off Succeed.

the hosts of Midian i.e. the rest of the village team and their supporters. The Midianites are often mentioned in the Old Testament as enemies of the Israelites.

to 'bag' the bowling i.e. to arrange to face as much of it as possible himself.

We've got to get ... get him out The repetition emphasizes Trimingham's determination.

fairy ring Circle of darker grass superstitiously believed by some to have been caused by fairies dancing.

Yet when I saw ... in hand After every ten runs the total is displayed on the simple scoreboard.

saw the field breaking up i.e. Leo sees the fielders leaving their set positions as the match is over.

didn't you keep one i.e. didn't you record full details of the match ... ?

C. sub Abbreviation of 'caught by substitute fielder'.

Chapter 13

At the supper in the village hall that evening, Mr Maudsley makes a witty speech in which he praises nearly all the players individually. When he mentions the match-winning catch,

Ted Burgess winks at Leo. The speeches are followed by songs, accompanied on the piano by Marian. Ted sings two songs and is obviously ill at ease when acknowledging the applause with Marian. Leo admires Marian's playing and is himself called on to sing. He enjoys a tremendous success and is aware of feeling at one with Marian as he sings. When he returns to his place he dozes off, waking to hear Marian singing 'Home, Sweet Home'. On the way back to the hall Marcus teases Leo and speaks snobbishly about the villagers. He lets Leo into a secret by telling him that Marian's engagement to Trimingham will be announced at the forthcoming ball.

The village hall sequence is full of ironic innuendo, with the songs (see the notes below) at the centre of this. The main irony however is to be found in Leo's feelings, his feeling close to Marian. Her singing of the song requested by Trimingham shows her being compelled into conformity, and Marcus's snobbery and his confiding in Leo increases the sense of oppression we feel at the turn events have taken. There is something infinitely sad about Leo's triumph: it is the high watermark of his life at Brandham but it is also the beginning of his descent, his movement out of favour and into the dark night of rejection.

it seemed to me ... present at Leo's reaction contrasts sharply with that of the over-sophisticated Marcus later in the chapter (p.151).

hock-cup Fruit-flavoured drink containing hock, a German white wine.

though I communed ... in the flesh Good example of Hartley's quiet humour.

our young David ... with a catch Goliath, the gigantic champion of the Philistines, was killed by David, a young shepherd boy, who hit him with the first stone shot from his sling (1 Samuel, 17, 19–58).

The more clothes ... look a yokel Again Hartley emphasizes that Ted represents natural man. His clothes hamper him. Note also the contrast with Trimingham, the civilized aristocrat.

that he was seedy Colloquial term meaning that he did not feel well.

badgered Pestered.

(in spite of the perpetual sunshine ... white) At that time the whiteness of a lady's skin was a visible sign that she was able to pamper herself and live an idle life. Women who worked in the country would have a telltale suntan.

tin-pot Inferior, cheap.

When Ted Burgess was called upon ... hadn't heard Notice how this section dealing with Ted follows the description of Marian's playing, and the reference to the 'thoroughbred ... harnessed to a cart-horse'. At the end of the paragraph (p.144) Ted gets up clumsily and stumbles towards the dais. By these means Hartley draws attention to the social difference between the two characters while retaining the reader's sympathy for Ted.

she dog-eared the page i.e. she turned down the corner.

'Take a Pair of Sparkling Eyes' Song by Marco in *The Gondoliers* (1889), a comic opera by Gilbert and Sullivan. This song, like 'Home, Sweet Home' later in the chapter (p.149), is carefully chosen by Hartley to fit the situation in which class barriers prevent Ted and Marian from revealing their love. The second verse begins

Take a pretty little cot – [i.e. cottage]
Quite a miniature affair –
Hung about with trellised vine,

and contains the lines

Live to love and love to live ...
Fate has nothing more to give.

Balfe Michael William Balfe, born in Dublin in 1808, was a well-known composer of operas and operettas, including *The Bohemian Girl* (1843). He died in 1870.

It never occurred to me ... concert-room Ironic in view of later events.

the music of the spheres In ancient times the universe was believed to consist of a number of concentric hollow transparent globes on which were fixed the sun, moon, planets and certain stars. It was thought that these globes emitted harmonious sounds (the music of the spheres) as they revolved.

If it wasn't for the difference i.e. in their respective social positions.

For the second time ... as, the third time ... I should not The first time was when Leo was called on to field in the cricket match. The third time to which he refers here, with hindsight, is when he discovers Marian and Ted in the outhouse (Chapter 23, p.262).

The Minstrel Boy Song with words by the Irish poet, Thomas Moore (1779–1852).

Angels ever bright and fair Aria from *Theodora*, an oratorio by Handel, first performed in 1750.

Handel's George Frederick Handel (1685–1759), the German-born composer of operas and oratorios who settled in England in 1712 and became court composer.

Clad in robes of virgin white Note the ironic implications of the references to virginity when associated with Marian.

Home, Sweet Home Song from the opera *Clari* (1823), composed by Henry Rowley Bishop (1786–1855), with a libretto by the American actor and dramatist John Howard Payne (1791–1852).

boss shots Unsuccessful attempts (slang).

I remembered she was singing ... request At Lord Trimingham's request (See Chapter 11, pp.122 and 125.)

Lor lumme i.e. Lord love me. Used facetiously by Leo.

made me go all goosy i.e. made me come out in goose flesh.

plebs People of the lower classes (slang). Abbreviation of plebeians.

cat Vomit (slang).

pi Pious (slang).

blub Colloquial term for cry, weep.

that I should fall down dead ... binding Another example of Hartley's dry humour.

Chapter 14

On Sunday morning Leo reflects delightedly on his triumphs of the previous day, and is also deeply satisfied by the thought that Marian is to marry Trimingham. He believes that he will no longer have to act as messenger for Ted and Marian, and looks forward to taking up his old pursuits with Marcus. After breakfast Leo writes to his mother, informing her of recent events and asking her to let him stay at Brandham for another week. He posts the letter and then goes to church with the Hall party. Walking back from church with Trimingham, Leo asks him why there is no memorial tablet for the fifth Viscount, and learns that he was buried in France after being killed in a duel over his wife. Leo realizes that the situation involving Ted, Marian and the Trimingham resembles that which caused the death of the fifth Viscount, but he does not dwell on the idea. He is impressed when Trimingham tells him that nothing is ever a lady's fault, and that the Boers have to be killed as a matter of military necessity, not because of personal dislike.

Leo contemplates life in all innocence, unaware (as ever) of the complexities and the misery to come). In this illusory state he asks to stay longer, a tragi-comic request in the light of forthcoming events. Trimingham's revelation in fact registers strongly with Leo, who makes the connection without for one moment understanding the full significance of it – thus he passes on to Trimingham's chivalrous conception of women and his attitude towards the Boer War, both of which reflect the studied cover-up rather than any emotional involvement. But Leo cannot be expected to grasp the sophisticated reasons for these views. He learns so much, but he knows so little.

Jacob's ladder i.e. means of reaching blissful heights. In a dream Jacob saw a ladder between heaven and earth, with angels ascending and descending. See Genesis, 28, 12.

Icarus See our note p.18 on 'You flew too near to the sun ... scorched' (Prologue, p.20).

Jessop Gilbert Laird Jessop (1874–1955) played cricket for Cambridge University, Gloucestershire and England. He was the most consistent hitter of all time, and throughout his career scored at an average 79 runs an hour.

Of course his Lordship took the wicket The bowler off whose bowling a catch is taken receives the credit for the dismissal.

force majeure Irresistible compulsion, superior strength (French).

Married to her ... live there With money from the Maudsleys Trimingham will be able to move back into Brandham Hall, where he is now temporarily their guest.

lacuna Gap, blank.

shibboleths Means of testing whether a person belongs to one particular class or group. See Judges, 12, 5–6.

Chapter 15

After luncheon Marcus tells Leo that he will not be able to play with him that afternoon, as Marian has asked him to go to see Nannie Robson. Leo intends to visit the rubbish-heap, but first he goes to check the thermometer. He is indulging in sentimental fantasies about Marian when she comes upon him and asks him to take a letter to Ted. He is shocked to learn that she has not broken off the relationship with Ted now that she is engaged, but he cannot tell her this since he is not supposed to know about the engagement. When Marian loses her temper and suggests that he wants to be paid to act as a messenger, Leo snatches the letter from her and runs off. He cries when he thinks that Marian has only been pretending to like him so that he will take messages between Ted and her.

When he reaches the farm Leo finds Ted in the kitchen, about to clean his gun. Ted senses that a woman has made Leo cry and tries to cheer him up. He takes him outside to watch him shoot and then shows him how to clean a gun and hold it for firing. Leo oils Ted's bat for him and gives him Marian's letter. He then agrees to take a message to Marian if Ted will tell him about 'spooning'. Ted tries to divert Leo from the topic, and will not give him specific information. When Leo threatens not to take any more messages unless he tells him all the facts, Ted loses his temper and orders him to get out.

The Nannie Robson visit is fraught with consequences. Marian makes further inroads into Leo's feelings when she again asks him to take a letter. Part of Leo's character is his conventional morality – not surprising in view of his upbringing – and this is evident here when he knows that Marian is betraying Trimingham by the mere fact of writing to Ted. He is deeply wounded when Marian is revealed in her true light, and sees into the heart of her motives when she loses her temper and her verbal control. The gun sequence with Ted is also full of foreboding – it looks forward to what happens off narrative after the end of the main sequence in *The Go-Between*. The pathos continues with Ted's failure to communicate the facts of life, his loss of temper corresponding to Marian's, both reflecting their frustration at the thought of not being able to go on making love, the 'spooning' plus of which Leo is ignorant. So on two occasions in this chapter Leo is on the receiving end for what he doesn't know and what he can't help.

zounds Abbreviation of 'by God's wounds', an archaic oath. Used facetiously by Marcus.
bally Mild form of bloody (slang).
giving such an easy score i.e. allowing myself to be scored off so easily.

Ministering Children A book of highly moral stories by Maria Louisa Charlesworth. Published in 1854, it had sold more than 12,000 copies by 1870.

would swallow a camel ... gnat See Matthew, 23, 24.

The iron curtain of secrecy ... holes Leo has promised Marcus not to reveal that he knows about Marian's engagement (Chapter 13, p.152).

Shylock Jewish moneylender in Shakespeare's *The Merchant of Venice.*

ugly duckling ... swan Reference to a fairy-tale by the Danish writer Hans Christian Andersen (1805–75).

a put-up job Something deceitfully concocted.

The muzzle was just below ... chest Foreshadows Ted's horrific death. See Epilogue, pp.263–4.

as if my salvation lay in shooting Ironic. Ted's death is, with the discovery in the outhouse, to cause Leo to become an emotional cripple in later life.

the bow of Ulysses Ulysses, the king of Ithaca in Greek legend, owned a bow that only he was capable of drawing.

to face the music i.e. to confront unpleasant consequences.

L.R.A.M. Abbreviation of Licentiate of the Royal Academy of Music.

Revision questions on Chapters 11–15

1 What do we learn about Mr Maudsley from his behaviour at the cricket match and the concert in the village hall?

2 In what ways do the cricket match and the concert bring out the differences in social class which Hartley wishes to emphasize?

3 How do the songs sung at the village hall supper contribute to Hartley's overall message in *The Go-Between*?

4 What impression do you get of Trimingham in these chapters?

5 Give an account of Leo's reactions to Marian and Ted in Chapter 15.

Chapter 16

The chapter begins with Leo's second letter that day to his mother. In it he tells her that he is no longer enjoying himself and asks her to send a telegram calling him home. After running out of Ted's kitchen Leo had returned to the Hall, where he was just in time for tea. In the absence of Mrs Maudsley, Marian had presided over the teacups and had behaved charmingly to Leo. After tea he had ignored Marian's unspoken message to stay behind, and had gone to write his letter. The chapter ends with a conversation between Leo and Trimingham, in which Leo learns that Marian is leaving the next day for a short stay in London, and that Mrs Maudsley is unwell. Trimingham also tells Leo that, according to Marian, her old nurse Nannie Robson is losing her memory and cannot remember whether she has been to see her or not.

Leo's sensitivity is shown in his sudden wish to leave Brandham Hall in view of the turn events have taken. Marian is of course betraying herself by trying to win Leo back, and all the pointers and undercurrents of this chapter indicate crisis – the mention of Nannie Robson, the illness of Mrs Maudsley, and Marian's going to London.

his gun, which I had ... symbol of himself The gun can be seen as a phallic symbol.
And Lord Trimingham ... the victim This is to prove true, but not in the way that Leo envisages.
amour propre Self-esteem (French).
as Marian had said before him See Chapter 15, p. 165.
she says the old girl's ... not Compare with Marcus's statement in Chapter 17, p.188.

Chapter 17

On his way to the rubbish-dump Leo meets Marcus, who insists on speaking in French and wants to go somewhere else. They head towards the outhouses. As they near their objective they discover a female footprint, and in the course of conversation Marcus reveals that his mother is afraid that Marian will break her engagement. He worries Leo further when he tells him that Marian had not arrived at Nannie Robson's house by the time he left and that the old woman has a good memory, contrary to the impression Marian had given to Trimingham. Marcus informs Leo that Marian is going to

London to buy clothes and to get him a green bicycle as a birthday present; but Leo's pleasure is blunted by the revelation that Marian thinks that green is his true colour. Seeking revenge, he tells Marcus that he knows where Marian is. When they reach the outhouses Leo sees that the deadly nightshade plant has grown tremendously since his last visit. Then the boys hear voices, one of which Leo recognizes as that of Ted Burgess. He manages to get Marcus away from the vicinity. The chapter ends with Leo's thoughts returning to the bicycle Marian intends to give him. He is greatly tempted to destroy the letter he has just written to his mother, remain at the Hall, and have the bicycle; but he decides to let the letter be collected from the box the following morning.

(*Note*: Much of the dialogue between Leo and Marcus in this chapter is written in French of a kind, with English interpolations. In translating the speeches the main intention has been to capture the spirit of what is said.)

Much is explained in Marcus's reference to the possible broken engagement and in his emphasis that Nannie Robson's memory is all right. The pieces of the jig-saw are beginning to fit in Leo's mind. The news of the green bicycle is offensive to Leo as I have indicated in the summary, but of course it indicates further duplicity on Marian's part – either a grim joke against Leo or her determination to use him for as long as he stays as a messenger. Moved to thoughts of temporary revenge, Leo as usual gives way to greater thoughts of decency, preventing Marcus from interrupting the lovers. This is an anticipation, with differences, of Mrs Maudsley's final journey with Leo when the lovers are discovered together.

Je le trouve ... ennuyeux I find it too boring.
pidgin French Form of French incorporating jargon, words from other languages etc.
Je suggère que nous ... outhouses I suggest that we visit the outhouses.
Mais oui! ... places delicieuses Yes. What a good idea! They are delightful places.
Vous venez sur You're coming on.
Et que trouvons-nous là And what shall we find there?
Eh bien, je jamais Well, I never!

Je vois l'empreinte ... pied I see a footprint.

Je dirai ... de Man Friday I shall tell Mother that we have seen
Man Friday's tracks. (In the novel *Robinson Crusoe* by Daniel
Defoe – 1660–1731 – the young savage, Man Friday, was found
by Crusoe on what he had believed to be a deserted island.)

Ou Mademoiselle Friday Or Miss Friday.

Certes, c'est la patte ... voleurs Yes, indeed, it is a woman's
footprint. What a mystery! What will Mother say? She is very
afraid of burglars! (The fact that Marcus identifies the footprint
as a woman's prepares the reader for the discovery of Marian in
the outhouse, p.192.)

Mais non! ... hystérique No, she is very highly-strung. She is a
rather hysterical person.

En ce moment ... de strain Right now she is in bed with a bad
migraine, the result of all these days of strain.

Ce n'est pas seulement ... Marianne It's not only that. It's
Marian.

Il s'agit ... Marianne— It concerns the betrothal. My mother
isn't sure that Marian—

Vous avez vu votre soeur ... Robson Did you see your sister at
Nannie Robson's?

Mais non! Quand je suis ... fâcheuse No. When I left Marian
hadn't yet arrived. And poor Nannie Robson was quite upset.

perdu sa mémoire Lost her memory.

Sa mémoire est aussi ... la vôtre Her memory is as good as
mine, and a hundred times better than yours.

Pourquoi Why?

En part, parce que ... de vous Partly because, like all women,
she needs new clothes for the ball; but largely because of you.

Entendez-vous ... nigaud Do you hear, rascal? Do you
understand, booby?

their Danaan implication Their Greek implication. The allusion
is to a line in Virgil's *Aeneid*: 'Timeo Danaos, et dona ferentes.'
(I fear the Greeks even when they bring gifts.)

les petits garçons Little-boys.

Je jure I swear.

C'est une bicyclette It's a bicycle.

Oombaire Marcus's pronunciation of 'Humber'.

Je ne sais pas I don't know.

Je ne l'ai pas vue I have not seen it

Vert – un vert vif Green, a bright green.

Et savez-vous pourquoi And do you know why?

Mais oui! Vraiment Yes, really!

Savez-vous où est Marian ... moment-ci Do you know where
Marian is now?

Oui ... sais bien I really do know.

Pas cent lieues d'ici Not a hundred leagues from here.
Je ne dis pas ... pas savoir I don't tell that to little boys. Little
  boy, little boy, wouldn't you like to know?
If I had remembered what a tell-tale ... whereabouts Leo
  realizes later that Marcus must have told Mrs Maudsley that
  he, Leo, knew where Marian was. See Epilogue, pp.266–7.
bold black burnished berries Effective use of alliteration.
It was the voice ... of his being The boys overhear Ted
  persuading Marian to let him make love to her.
un couple qui fait le cuiller A couple 'spooning'.
Mais non! ... faire! No, that would be too boring. Let's leave
  them to it!
Jurez ... en prie Swear that you won't, please.
Cela dépend That depends.
skivvies Derogatory term for female domestic servants.
Deux mois, trois mois Two months, three months.
folle—fou Both words mean mad.
hush-money Money (or in this case a present) given to someone
  in exchange for keeping quiet about something.
Vous êtes ... votre voix You are very quiet. I don't like your
  voice.
Et quant ... langue And as for your nasty thoughts, toad, I
  don't care a rap for them, I spit (upon them). But why have you
  lost your tongue?

Chapter 18

The next morning Leo is relieved to find that his letter has
been taken. Breakfast is a relaxed occasion, as Mrs Maudsley
is ill in bed and Marian has caught the early train to London
with four of the weekend visitors. Monday and Tuesday are
two of the happiest days of Leo's stay at Brandham Hall,
largely owing to the lack of organized activities. The temperature is rising again, but the weather is more settled. Leo looks
forward to receiving the telegram from his mother that will
signal his release. On Tuesday morning he gets a letter from
Ted Burgess, apologizing for losing his temper when they last
met and inviting Leo to visit him on the following Sunday,
when he will tell him about 'spooning'. Leo suspects Ted's
motives for writing, but believes that in any case he will be
back with his mother before Sunday. He seeks out Trimingham in the smoking-room to ask him about a phrase in Ted's
letter that he cannot understand. Trimingham tells him that

Ted is 'a bit of a lady-killer', but Leo does not know what this means. When Mr Maudsley joins them Trimingham informs him that he has spoken to Ted about joining up, and he tells Leo that it is 'on the cards' that Ted will go to the war. As Leo is leaving he overhears Mr Maudsley saying that Ted has a woman in the vicinity, but Leo does not understand the expression.

This is a tranquil chapter in the first instance, Hartley employing a period of calm before the storm, metaphorical and factual, breaks. But the plot now moves on with Trimingham's account of his meeting with Ted: in simple language, Ted is being got out of the way. The main ironic current of the chapter is the adult male conversation, filled with sexual innuendo, which even at this stage Leo does not understand.

The cats were away Allusion to the proverb, 'When the cat's away, the mice will play.' The small group at breakfast feel at their ease, particularly with Mrs Maudsley absent.

ushers Old-fashioned term for assistant teachers.

sacked Dismissed (slang).

impots Impositions, work set as punishment at school (slang).

'awe' is a rude word Marcus confuses 'awe' with 'whore'.

familiar Demon attending on and serving a witch. Appropriate in view of the way in which Marian has enchanted Leo.

I got my rag out i.e. I lost my temper (slang).

smoking-room stories Improper anecdotes.

I thought ... above his head i.e. I thought he might not understand them.

joining up Enlisting in the armed forces.

N.C.O. Abbreviation for non-commissioned officer.

since Roberts went into Pretoria Lord Roberts occupied the Boer capital, Pretoria, on 5 June 1900.

the Transvaal Province of South Africa lying to the north of the Vaal River.

it's on the cards i.e. it is quite likely.

Chapter 19

Leo is not worried when the expected telegram fails to arrive by 11.15 in the morning and he spends most of the day with Marcus who tells him about the arrangements for the ball and for his birthday. At six o'clock on Friday, Marian intends to ride the green bicycle into the tea party, but Leo believes he will have left Brandham by then. A telegram arrives, but it is from Marian, not from Leo's mother, and he convinces himself that his mother will write rather than waste money on a telegram. On Wednesday morning there is still no communication from Leo's mother. He thinks he will be leaving on the following day, but wonders if the Maudsleys will insist on his staying until Friday, in which case he might get the bicycle. He decides to visit Ted to say good-bye. Informing Marcus that Ted has promised to give him a swimming lesson, he sets off towards the farm. Ted is driving the reaper, but comes over to talk to Leo, who tells him he will be leaving shortly. Ted wishes him good luck and Leo asks him if it is true that he is going to the war, receiving the reply that it depends on what Marian wants. Leo is moved at parting from Ted, and offers to take one more message to Marian. Ted tells him to say that ' he will meet her on Friday at half-past six at the usual place.

Leo is bolstered by the fact that the telegram will arrive, but the reader is aware of the mounting external tension which he cannot read. His decision to visit Ted is the turning point of his life: again we are aware of his decent motives, but these lead him into the trap of playing go-between again. He is unwittingly the maker of his own tragedy – and Friday when he will receive the green bicycle is the crucial day arranged for the meeting between Ted and Marian. The pace of the plot is quickening.

that wonder ... nine days A nine days' wonder is a novelty that attracts a lot of attention but is soon forgotten.
Contrary to the proverb ... much Allusion to the proverb, 'Tell no tales out of school.'
crétin Idiot (French).
il est un peu ... savez It's rather provincial, you know. (French).
give it out i.e. announce it.
mais les chandelles But the candles (French). See Chapter 23, p.257.
saignant Bloody (French).
baker's dozen Thirteen.
clou Star turn, main attraction (French).
bloomers Loose knee-length trousers worn by women.
not quite-quite i.e. socially unacceptable.
Battersea District of London, lying on the south bank of the Thames.

owl Used here to mean a solemn-looking stupid person.

Pas comme ... défendu Not proper – absolutely forbidden (French).

Claude Claude Gellés (1600–82) – known in English as Claude or Claude Lorraine – was a French landscape painter.

déranger Disturb (French).

Punch Humorous illustrated weekly magazine founded in 1841.

Mr Punch ... Dog Toby Mr Punch, a hunch-back with a hook nose, appeared in the traditional Punch and Judy show with Dog Toby, a trained dog wearing a frill round its neck. Both characters were taken over by *Punch* magazine, for its illustrated cover.

Lord Methuen The 3rd Baron Methuen (1845–1932) served in the Boer War from 1899 to 1902, and commanded the 1st Division of the 1st Army Corps.

in a hole and corner fashion i.e. in a secret and underhand way.

un petit quart d'heure A few minutes (French).

façon de parler Manner of speaking (French).

I wrote right off i.e. I wrote immediately.

As I was turning away, grieved The depth of Leo's attachment to Ted is shown by the use of 'grieved' here and elsewhere in the novel. See Chapter 21, p.231, and Epilogue, p.263.

Chapter 20

At teatime Leo receives his mother's letter, but contrary to his expectations, she tells him that she wants him to stay at Brandham Hall. The letter makes him feel confused, and he wanders about the outbuildings and visits the rubbish-heap. He is chiefly anxious to avoid being alone with Marian. On Thursday morning Mrs Maudsley comes down to breakfast, and the atmosphere is less relaxed than it has been in her absence. Marian catches Leo as he is leaving the room, and from the conversation that follows it is obvious that she is unhappy. When Leo lets it slip that Trimingham has asked Ted to join up she is furious, saying that she will tell Trimingham she will not marry him if Ted goes to the war. Leo asks her why she does not marry Ted, but she says that it is impossible and bursts into tears. Leo's feelings of regard for Marian revive and he weeps in sympathy. When she asks him if he has a message for her he passes it on, but alters the time of the proposed meeting to six o'clock, hoping in this way to break the relationship between Ted and Marian.

With his mother's letter counselling the reverse of what he thinks he wants, Leo drops his guard when he tells Marian that Ted may join the army. It sparks the crisis which has been waiting for ignition. Marian's tears of course so move Leo that he is now defenceless, but his reflex determination to end the relationship between Ted and Marian forces him to change the time of their meeting – again evidence of his immaturity and the fact that he too has been corrupted into deception by the example of Ted and Marian.

Fordingbridge Small town eleven miles south of Salisbury.

knocks one up i.e. exhausts one, makes one feel ill.

All this will be an *experience* ... darling Note the unconscious irony of this statement.

non-conductor Scientific term meaning something that does not conduct or transmit.

slanging you i.e. using abusive language to you.

I guesses then ... real bed Marian means the lot that has been chosen for her – marrying a man she does not love.

Jingo Supporter of aggressive policies in the interests of one's country.

But Friday at six o'clock Leo alters the time in Ted's message (see Chapter 19, p.217). His reason for doing so is given in Chapter 21 (p.232).

You're a friend ... thousand We remember these words, together with the kiss and tears that precede them, when Leo meets Marian again in the Epilogue (p.280).

Revision questions on Chapters 16–20

1 How far do you feel sympathetic to Marian in these chapters?

2 Write an account of how Hartley maintains tension in Chapter 17.

3 In what ways does Hartley underline the opposition between Ted and Trimingham in the smoking-room scene in Chapter 18?

4 'All this will be an *experience* for you, my darling.' How do you respond to the unintended irony in Mrs Colston's letter in Chapter 20?

Chapter 21

Although Leo is reconciled with Marian he still has reservations about her behaviour. He worries about the consequences of her relationships with the two men, and determines to do what he can to break the spell he believes Ted has cast on Marian. Already he has told her the wrong time for the assignation with Ted on Friday. Now he will go a stage further by concocting a spell that will destroy Ted's influence over Marian. That night Leo creeps out of the hall and visits the outhouse where the deadly nightshade grows. He intends to break off parts of the plant to use in his spell. When he gets to the outhouse the deadly nightshade seems to reach out towards him. He enters the shed, but panics when the plant brushes against his face. He tears at it and finally uproots it, chanting 'Delenda est belladonna!' as he does so.

Leo's reversion to thinking in terms of breaking the spell (ironic, in view of the fact that the spell is one of sexual potency) shows how really young he is. The deadly nightshade is symbolic of corruption, evil, destruction, and the fear which Leo shows is consonant with his fears of what he has been doing for Marian and Ted. The scene in the shed is charged with supernatural force, and Leo's vulnerability is again revealed.

call him out i.e. challenge him to a duel.
AB, BC, CA Leo sees Marian, Ted and Trimingham as members of an eternal triangle (a situation involving both men and Marian in problems caused by the conflict in her feelings).
reproaches ... rupture Effective use of alliteration.
gathering A swelling containing pus.
naphtha flare A kind of oil-fired light.
Il faut en finir i.e. it must be ended (French).
A Midsummer Night's Dream Play by Shakespeare in which, while they are asleep, several characters are put under a spell that causes them to fall in love with the first living creature seen on waking. When the spell is reversed they remember almost nothing of what has happened.
Puck Mischievous fairy who is the servant of Oberon, king of the fairies, in *A Midsummer Night's Dream*.
Jaeger dressing-gown i.e. one made from woollen material.
The Thorn Song composed by William Shield (1748–1829), with words by the Irish playwright, John O'Keefe (1747–1833).

No trowel or spade ... in case of fire Leo has already
  described his plan as 'a chemistry experiment' (p.238). This
  section and the paragraph beginning 'Then having arrived'
  (p.239) are written in a style often thought to be appropriate for
  recording a scientific experiment.
alembic Piece of apparatus formerly used in distilling.
At that I panicked ... way out Hartley here conveys the degree
  of Leo's terror by his deliberately clumsy repetition of 'way out'.
delenda est belladonna The belladonna must be destroyed!
  (Latin).
coronal Wreath, garland.

Chapter 22

Leo is still asleep when the footman wakes him up on the morning of his birthday. The skies threaten rain. Leo dismantles
the equipment he used for his attempts at magic the night
before, and prepares to face reality now that he is thirteen.
Abandoning the green suit he goes down to breakfast wearing
a Norfolk jacket, and receives congratulations on his birthday.
He opens two envelopes that have arrived from his mother
and his aunt. Each contains a tie and a letter. When Leo takes
out the tie from his aunt it is doubtfully received by the
company on account of its colour and because it is already
made up into a bow, but Trimingham takes it from him and
puts it on to remove any possible embarrassment Leo might
be feeling. Mrs Maudsley gives Leo the chance to choose how
to spend the day, but succeeds in organizing things to suit
herself. A visit to Beeston Castle is provisionally arranged for
after luncheon, and Leo is to cut his birthday cake at five o'clock.
He spends the morning with Marcus, and before luncheon
changes into his green suit, after which he feels more normal.

The chapter is full of portents – the change in the weather,
Mrs Maudsley's getting to grips with the day, Leo's donning
his green suit, the kindness of Trimingham and the ritual of
family performance and snobbery. Leo, despite being made to
feel relaxed, is always the outsider in this close-knit and self-
protective group.

Good morning ... happy returns Particularly ironic in view of
  the effect the day's events are to have on Leo's life.

The Dog Days That part of July and August believed from ancient times to be the hottest and most unpleasant period of the year.

temenos Sacred enclosure (Greek).

Olympian Condescending, superior.

mumbo-jumbo Meaningless ritual.

quackery Charlatanism, pretence of having skill.

he would much rather tell ... happened Ironic. Marcus's lack of discretion is the chief factor that betrays Marian to Mrs Maudsley. See Epilogue, pp.266–7.

motley Literally means 'a jester's uniform'. Used here to show that in wearing the suit Leo feels free to adopt a different personality.

Liverpool Street London railway terminus for trains from Norwich.

outré Beyond the bounds of what is usually thought proper (French).

a made-up tie i.e. one with the bow already tied. The snobbish Marcus has shown his disapproval earlier when Leo opened the envelope containing the tie (p.248).

Chapter 23

After luncheon the sky looks ominous and Mrs Maudsley suggests waiting a quarter of an hour before making a decision about the afternoon excursion. Marian takes Leo outside and tries to pass him a letter for Ted; but they are interrupted by her mother, who sees Marian stuff the letter into Leo's pocket, saying that it is a note telling Nannie Robson that she will visit her that afternoon. Mrs Maudsley forces Leo to take a walk in the gardens with her, in the course of which she traps him into revealing that he does not know where Nannie Robson lives, and tries to make him tell her to whom he has previously taken messages for Marian. The interrogation is ended when it starts to rain heavily. Later that afternoon, at Leo's birthday tea, Mrs Maudsley behaves charmingly to him. Marian is the only absentee. The guests believe she is at Nannie Robson's, and as it is raining hard Mr Maudsley sends a carriage to bring her back. The cake is cut and crackers are being pulled when the butler enters to inform Mrs Maudsley that Marian has not been to Nannie Robson's. Mrs Maudsley's nerve cracks and, grabbing Leo, she sets off to find her daughter.

She appears to know where she is and, through the pouring rain, leads Leo to the outhouses. He tries to divert her from the area, but she compels him to go with her into a shed where they see Ted and Marian making love. Mrs Maudsley begins to scream hysterically. The chapter ends with the elderly Leo saying that while he was still at Brandham Hall he learned that Ted Burgess had gone home and shot himself.

This is the climactic chapter of the novel. Mrs Maudsley turns detective with frightening efficiency, and the pace of the narrative leaves no time for inaction. What stands out is the sacrifice of Leo, made the scapegoat by Mrs Maudsley and subjected to the sight of something he has never understood – the name and nature of 'spooning' in all its immediate physicality. Mrs Maudsley has solved the mystery at terrible cost to herself and, more particularly we may feel, at inexcusable cost to Leo. The graphic terror he feels has a terrible footnote – the suicide of Ted Burgess. The class barriers have been preserved: Leo's life – and Ted's – have been wrecked. There is personal, moral and social comment in this fine ending.

Well, not quite, but I can ask On his later visit to Brandham the elderly Leo recalls this moment. See Epilogue, p.275.

But I remember running ... person In this section Hartley skilfully reinforces the idea of Leo's isolation. His mother has insisted on his staying at the Hall; Marian is making use of him; Mrs Maudsley has subjected him to a severe interrogation; and now he finds himself ousted from his room.

He's a regular ... didn't answer Lord Trimingham's joking remark is not taken up by Mrs Maudsley, who knows that another 'lady's man' is 'Marian's cavalier'.

brougham Closed carriage drawn by one horse.

I was rather breathless ... blow Indicates the tension Leo is feeling, as does the fact that he cannot swallow his piece of cake.

languishing voices chanted ... rhymes People are reading aloud from mottoes found in the crackers.

hobgoblin look i.e. resemblance to imps or bogymen. Note how the whole description emphasizes distortion, thereby reflecting Leo's extreme anxiety.

newel-post Post that supports the stair-handrail.

dunce's cap A conical paper hat, which used to be placed on a schoolchild's head as a sign of disgrace if he was unsuccessful at his lessons. Note the irony in Hartley's choice of hat for Leo. He has been slow to learn his lesson about Ted and Marian, but is on the point of receiving instant knowledge of the facts of life when he and Mrs Maudsley discover the lovers.

We saw them ... moving like one Leo and Mrs Maudsley see Marian and Ted in the act of making love.

Epilogue

The Epilogue is set in 1952. The elderly Leo finds that recording the events of 1900 has not stopped their troubling him, and he decides to revisit Brandham to find out what happened after he left. The immediate result of the discovery of Ted and Marian had been that Leo had suffered a breakdown. Believing that he had betrayed everyone, he felt vanquished, and shrank into himself. When he returned to school he and Marcus were distant towards each other, and Leo developed an interest in facts rather than people. The older Leo finds an unopened, unaddressed letter among his papers, and guesses that it is the one that Marian had wanted him to take to Ted on the afternoon of his birthday. When he reads it he learns that Marian was going to give him the bicycle so that he could take her messages more easily.

When Leo goes back to Brandham he heads for the church, where he finds memorial tablets to Hugh Trimingham and his son, the tenth Viscount, who was born less than seven months after Leo had left Brandham Hall in 1900. Realizing that the eleventh Viscount might still be alive, Leo leaves the church after praying for those who had been involved in the dramatic events. He meets the eleventh Viscount and realizes from his colouring that he is descended from Ted Burgess. Lord Trimingham tells him that Marian is still alive, and arranges for him to call on her. Marian, who is now living in Nannie Robson's house, is a lonely old woman, hurt by the reluctance of her grandson to visit her because he feels tainted by the events of long ago. In conversation with Leo she tells him what happened after she was discovered with Ted, and shows that she is self-deluded about the impact the events of that summer had on other people. Finally, Marian persuades Leo to tell her grandson that there was nothing shameful about her love for Ted, and that he must feel free to marry. Although he has long since decided never again to be a go-between, Leo sets off to the Hall with this last message.

Leo's interest in facts enables him to play the detective here. His discovery that Marian had Ted's son moves him to wish to see Marian. But she, unable to live as she feels she ought to be living, idealises the past and shows herself a sad and deluded woman. Her life too has been wrecked, though we feel that there is much self-blame attached to this. The final sequence with Leo as Mercury again is full of the author's irony. Leo, too young to know, is apparently too old to learn, and his heart, untouched for 52 years, gives in once more.

Pascal Blaise Pascal (1623–62) was a French philosopher, scientist, mathematician and writer.

the First War i.e. the First World War (1914–18).

to lay some unction ... soul i.e. to soothe my wounded feelings. Hartley is here adapting a line from *Hamlet*, III, 4, 145.

Bluebeard's chamber Meaning here 'location of terrible secrets'. Bluebeard was the villain of a tale published in 1697: he killed six wives who disobeyed his order not to look into a locked room in his castle.

vis-à-vis With regard to: literally, 'face to face with' (French).

Defying augury ... Maid's Head Leo defies a bad omen by staying at the Norwich hotel where he and Marian lunched over fifty years before. (See Chapter 4, p.47.) Hartley's line echoes *Hamlet*, V, 2, 211.

revenant One returned from the dead, or from exile etc.

Requiescat May he rest (Latin).

though I could not ... prayer Many clergymen will not allow the body of anyone who has committed suicide to be buried in consecrated ground.

I remembered his colouring ... May cf. Chapter 9, p.101.

Ancient Mariner Reference to the poem by Samuel Taylor Coleridge (1772–1834), in which the old mariner delays a wedding guest by his lengthy narrative.

It might have ... there had been Leo means that Ted and Marian would have been able to arrange to meet without involving him in carrying messages.

I thought of ... done so i.e. when he and Mrs Maudsley caught her with Ted.

taking pot-luck i.e. accepting whatever has been prepared.

Your grandfather used ... meeting In this section Leo twice mentions the eleventh Viscount Trimingham's grandfather, but notice that he is referring to both Hugh and Ted. Compare the first reference with Chapter 14, p.161; and the second with Chapter 19, pp.215–17.

remembering his grandfather's contrition Ted carried his contrition to the lengths of shooting himself.

like poor old Nannie Robson used to Marian used to tell others that Nannie Robson was forgetful; now she appears to have deceived herself into believing her own lies.

waited till it all blew over i.e. waited until the scandal died down.

the Dower House House provided for the widow of a nobleman when the inheritor of the title takes over the main family residence.

Oh, poor Mama! ... go away Finding Marian with Ted drove Mrs Maudsley mad, and she had to be sent to an asylum.

we couldn't have carried on Marian means that she and Ted could not have continued meeting without Leo's help, but the double meaning in the phrase 'carried on' is evident.

Revision questions on Chapter 21–Epilogue

1 Indicate in what ways Hartley raises tension in the encounter between Leo and the deadly nightshade plant in Chapter 21.

2 'Now that I was thirteen I was under an obligation to look reality in the face.' (Chapter 22.) How true does this prove to be for Leo?

3 Do you feel more sympathy for Mrs Maudsley or for Leo in Chapter 23, when Leo is forced by Mrs Maudsley to take her to the outhouses where Marian is making love with Ted?

4 Leo has been destroyed by his experiences at Brandham Hall in 1900. Write notes on your reactions to Marian's interpretation of earlier events when she meets him again in 1952.

The characters

Leo Colston

I carried about with me something that made me dangerous,
but what it was and why it made me dangerous, I had no idea.

Leo Colston, the 'go-between' of the title, is the narrator of the
novel. He is seen mainly as a schoolboy in 1900 when he is just
approaching his thirteenth birthday, but in the Prologue and
Epilogue he appears as a man in his sixties. His adult life has
been scarred by the shock of the events of 1900, when he was
involved in a sexual intrigue at Brandham Hall in Norfolk
where he had been invited to be a guest of the Maudsley
family. In the Prologue and Epilogue we learn that after his
experiences at Brandham Leo has settled for a life of *facts*. He
sets out on a journey into his past, to try to make sense of what
happened – and, indirectly to make sense of his own life.

Young Leo is the only child of a widow who lives in a village
near Salisbury; she is not well off, but is able to send him away
to school. Leo has no reason to be vain about his appearance,
but is conceited about other things, in particular his command
of language and what he conceives to be a power over events –
as reflected by the seeming effectiveness of the curses he uses
against his enemies at school. In addition, Leo has great hopes
of the twentieth century – in a wider sense as well as for
himself – and he constructs a fantasy round the figures of the
zodiac decorating the diary for 1900 that his mother has given
to him. His mistake is to continue to believe that he can
influence events when he is invited to Brandham Hall in the
summer; and to look too closely for parallels between the
people he meets on his visit and the figures of the zodiac.
Particularly in the case of Marian, the connection with the
signs of the zodiac is ironic.

Leo is an outsider at Brandham Hall, whee he finds himself
in a different kind of society from that of his home. He becomes
somewhat infected by snobbishness, which shows itself when
he learns that Trimingham is a viscount. And he becomes a
great supporter of the values the Hall represents, though he

finds it impossible to share his friend Marcus's scorn for those lower in the social scale.

At first Leo spends most of his time in the company of Marcus, and they occupy themselves in boyish pursuits. Leo has come to Norfolk without any summer clothes and, because he is uncomfortable, he tries casting a spell in the hope of bringing the temperature down. The spell does not succeed, and this is the first sign that Leo will not be able to exert power over events at Brandham Hall. After his visit to Norwich in Marian's company Leo becomes infatuated with her in an unrealistic way. He is sexually immature and is unaware of the ways in which lovers behave. Nevertheless, he feels jealousy and possessiveness about Marian; and in the course of the novel reacts against both Trimingham and Ted because they threaten to take her from him. In each case, however, Leo's attitude is complicated by the admiration he feels for these men.

Leo is a sensitive, introverted character who is deeply concerned with problems of moral responsibility. He is, 'like [his] mother, sometimes up and sometimes down'. He is easily elated, as when Trimingham dignifies him with the name of Mercury. But he is as easily put down, for example when Marian calls him a Shylock and Ted Burgess chases him out of his kitchen. He is upset when he discovers that the messages he has been carrying are love letters, and is desolated at the thought that Marian has not lived up to his ideal vision of her. But he recognizes the strength of the attraction between Ted and Marian, and continues to love her, pouring out his soul for her in song when she accompanies him on the piano at the concert.

Leo's sensitivity is wide ranging, For example, he feels for Lord Trimingham and tries to soften the blow when Marian is cruel to him; and he is upset to see Ted Burgess suffering on account of his love for Marian when he visits him for the last time. Leo also finds himself deeply moved when Marian weeps over her hopeless love for Ted, even after he has decided that she cannot be trusted. Nevertheless, it is Leo's very sensitivity that provokes the violent climax of the novel. He has been hit on the raw when Marcus reveals that Marian thinks green is an appropriate colour for him and, to get back at her, reveals that he knows her whereabouts – a boast that Marcus conveys to his mother.

Reading the novel, it is easy to overlook how inadequately Leo's education and upbringing have prepared him for life. Adults treat him on equal terms, but he himself recognizes that he does not always understand what they are saying. In Marcus's company he reveals himself a schoolboy still, and on several occasions he tries to get away on his own to avoid the pressures crowding in upon him. Leo's inherent childishness is demonstrated by his rationalizations concerning his mother's failure to send him a telegram calling him back home; and, on his birthday, he is shown as a frightened child in the interview with Mrs Maudsley in the garden and during the tea party that afternoon. The final cruelty of being made to accompany Mrs Maudsley in her search for Marian is almost intolerable to read. The scene Leo then witnesses together with Ted's death and the strain he has been under for several weeks, causes him to have a breakdown from which he never fully recovers.

In the Epilogue the elderly Leo is shown as having lost the optimism he had felt at the beginning of the century. He finds 'so little room for praise or thanksgiving in the modern world', but prays for the souls of everyone involved in the drama at Brandham so long ago. When he meets Marian again he is amazed at the extent of her self-deception, but allows himself to be persuaded to tell the eleventh Viscount that there was nothing shameful about Marian's love for Ted Burgess. The fact that Leo decides to carry out Marian's request can be seen as a slightly hopeful sign. He is going to do something that will have a positive effect on Lord Trimingham, and indirectly on himself: he will be casting a vote in favour of life.

Marian Maudsley

'I expect you think me a ghastly old governess, don't you, slanging you and calling you names. But I'm not really – really I'm a good-natured girl.'

Marian is the character around whom the main action of the novel revolves. The conflict between her love affair with Ted Burgess and her engagement to Lord Trimingham leads to

Leo's involvement as a go-between; and to the final catastrophic discovery of the lovers in the outhouse. Apart from
Leo, Marian is the only character taking part in the events of
1900 to survive until 1952, the year of the Epilogue.

Marian enters the action of the novel in Chapter 2, when
Leo comes upon her unawares. Marcus has told him that she
is very beautiful, and he studies her closely in the light of this
announcement. Her beauty is obvious, but so is the formidable quality she inherits from her mother. The fact that the
Deadly Nightshade plant is described very soon afterwards
leads the reader to understand that Hartley is symbolically
pointing out that evil and beauty are to be expected within
Marian, just as they are to be found in the plant.

The mixture of qualities in the makeup of Marian's character affects Leo strongly. She wins a battle of wills with her
mother to take him on a shopping expedition to Norwich, and
from then onwards he is her devoted servant, linking her in his
mind with the figure of the Virgin in his fantasy of the zodiac.
He is delighted when she divines his secret that he has no
summer clothes at home, and the day spent in Norwich in her
company marks a a transformation for him in several ways; he
is able to put on the new clothes, which give him a sensation
of freedom; but Marian also awakens his adolescent sexual
instincts.

Marian takes advantage of Leo's malleability to make him
act as messenger between Ted and herself. On his return from
Black Farm with a cut knee she betrays great emotion when
Leo slips Ted's letter to her, but she deceives him by saying
that the messages to and from Ted concern business trans-
actions. Throughout the time that Leo is at Brandham Hall,
Marian's attitude towards him is never straightforward.
There is no doubt that she likes him, but she is ready to make
use of him. For example, the visit to Norwich is undertaken
partly to get clothes for him, but she has also planned things
so that she can meet Ted Burgess there. She buys him a
bicycle for a birthday present, but, as Leo learns from the
letter in the Epilogue, it was chosen with the idea of helping
him to take letters more easily to Ted. These are examples of
Marian being willing to use Leo deliberately, but on other
occasions she is unconscious of the effect that she is having on

him – for instance on the return from the bathing party when she seems to flirt with him as he touches her hair, which is drying on the bathing costume fastened round her neck – whereas in fact her excitement has been caused by Ted's presence at the bathing place.

Marian is able to hurt Leo deeply, as can be seen when she tells him she would be very angry if he were to tell anyone about the first letter he brings back from Ted. On seeing his reaction, she retracts her statement; but later in the book she causes him to cry when she rounds on him because of his refusal to take a letter to Ted when he knows that her engagement to Trimingham will shortly be announced. This is probably her cruellest action in the book, though she has previously shown how cutting she can be when she tells Leo to inform Trimingham she will sing at the village concert if he will do so as well.

These instances serve to show the difficult situation in which Marian finds herself: in love with Ted and unable to show it, while her mother is forcing her into a match she does not want. Her rebellion has to be channelled into her sexual relationship with Ted, which has to take place in hidden corners. She does not have sufficient daring to oppose her mother openly and admit her love for Ted – though enough has evidently been said for Mrs Maudsley to be afraid that Marian will not stick to her engagement. As it is, whenever Ted appears in the action of the novel at the same time as Marian, she has to suppress her feelings and pretend not to notice him. But Leo recognizes the depth of her involvement as he watches her while Ted is batting in the cricket match.

Marian's liveliness and independence of spirit are evident in many of her actions in the novel. In addition to crossing swords with her mother over the timing of the visit to Norwich, and over the question of putting off the ball if Marcus has got measles, she is the only person present at the concert in the village hall who is ready to play when the pianist fails to arrive, and she refuses to give an encore after she has sung. She seems ready to be angry with Trimingham when Leo is only made twelfth man in the Hall cricket team. And when she learns that Trimingham has tried to persuade Ted to enlist in the army she immediately thinks of telling him that she will not marry him if Ted joins up. Leo notices that, although he never hears her say a clever thing during his stay with the Maudsleys, she seems superior to everyone and possesses 'an air of good-humoured impatience with things and people'. He notes that Marian has 'her own angle on' the inhabitants of Brandham Hall, which is 'generally a slightly disconcerting one'. But with all her independent vision she lacks the willpower to jump the class barriers and marry Ted.

When, on his return to Brandham, the elderly Leo sees Marian he says that he would not have recognized her, though he remembers the hawk-like nose and fiery eyes. Leo finds that Marian is now living a lonely life in the Dower House. She tells Leo what happened after she was discovered with Ted in the outhouse, though it is evident from all she says that she has deceived herself about those events: she remembers everything in a way that reflects well on herself and shows little pity for the others involved. She only shows signs of being moved when she refers to her grandson, who seldom visits her; and she prevails upon Leo to let him know that her love for Ted was a beautiful thing, and to tell him that 'there's no spell or curse except an unloving heart.' Along with Leo, the reader marvels at Marian's capacity for self-deception, but is also moved by her evident love for her grandson – who would not exist had it not been for her illicit love affair of more than fifty years ago.

Ted Burgess

'Well, he's quite a decent feller ... but he's a bit wild.'

Ted Burgess is isolated from the other leading characters in *The Go-Between* on two counts; he is socially inferior to them, and is the only one to be totally destroyed when his affair with Marian is discovered, although Mrs Maudsley and Leo, though remaining alive, also suffer greatly.

Hartley makes use of the character of Ted in two main ways in the novel. He creates him to act as a contrast to Lord Trimingham (thereby throwing further light on class differences at the turn of the century), and also to raise questions of sexual and emotional development as they affect Leo. This should not be taken to imply that Ted is a cardboard figure –

on the contrary, in some ways he is the most vivid character in the book – but his place in the overall design of the novel should not be overlooked.

He makes his first appearance anonymously, as the man seen by Leo in the distance, raising his hat in farewell to Marian on the day she takes Leo to buy clothes in Norwich (Chapter 4, p.48). Later in Chapter 4 Leo first becomes aware of Ted as an individual when he sees him bathing in the river. Significantly, this happens very shortly after Marcus has spoken to Leo of the imminent arrival of Trimingham, who is seen by Mrs Maudsley as a potential husband for Marian. Leo is impressed by Ted's physique, and throughout the book he is to be associated with nature and what is natural. He works the land, in contrast to Trimingham who merely owns it. He is often linked with animals, and has a healthy regard for their sexuality and, by implication, his own. As Leo says, 'For him the word "natural" seemed to be conclusive' (Chapter 10, p.117).

Ted's attitude towards Leo is ambiguous. When he catches the boy sliding down his straw-stack he is angry, but relents when he learns that Leo is from the Hall. To some extent he treats Leo kindly, from self-interest because he can be used as a messenger; but there are several occasions when he seems to act towards him with genuine kindness. His angry response when Leo pushes things too far in trying to get Ted to explain 'spooning' is real enough, and his reactions to Leo's successes in the cricket match and at the concert are not fabricated. Ted is anxious for Leo to learn the facts of life in a way that will not be harmful to him. Ironically, he is finally responsible for stunting for all time Leo's growth in this direction.

Ted's love for Marian is presented by Hartley as genuine, though he has a reputation as a lady-killer. Trimingham and Mr Maudsley know that Ted has a weakness for women, and the fact is also commented on by the Maudsleys' coachman on the return from the picnic in Chapter 8. Ted himself grins when he tells Leo that his carriage horse is called Wild Oats, realizing the application of the name to his own activities, but when he believes that Marian may be going to marry Trimingham and leave him, it affects him physically. As Leo says, 'Sweating though he was, he looked dried up, the husk of the man he had been. He had taken in his belt another notch, I noticed' (Chapter 19, p.215).

The chapters dealing with the cricket match and the entertainment in the village hall provide a great deal of information about Ted. His rustic approach to batting is very effective, and it is only Leo's intervention that prevents his defeating Trimingham. He is uneasy in the village hall, wearing constricting clothes and having to conform to accepted norms of social behaviour, but when he takes a bow with Marian, one of the villagers comments, 'If it wasn't for the difference, what a handsome pair they'd make.' In environment of his own choosing Ted is supreme, and it is hard not to share Marian's anger on his behalf when Trimingham, from his superior social position, tries to get him to enlist in the army.

Ted is finally defeated by the prevailing class system. He is Trimingham's tenant farmer and knows that he can never be openly accepted as a suitor for Marian. Instead, he has to meet her in rotting outhouses, and is very aware that his decision whether or not to join the army depends on what she wants. Leo grieves deeply for Ted when he learns that he has shot himself, but Marian's cool assessment in the Epilogue is that he 'had a weak streak in him ... He should have waited till it all blew over ...'

Lord Trimingham

I felt that he had some inner reserve of strength which no reverse, however serious, would break down.

Hugh Winlove, ninth Viscount Trimingham, enters the novel in Chapter 5, having been mentioned in the previous two chapters. Hartley uses him as a contrast to Ted Burgess, and to illustrate class attitudes of the time (see *Themes*). He is the owner of Black Farm, and Ted Burgess is his tenant. He also owns Brandham Hall, which is let to the Maudsleys, as he doesn't have enough money to live in it himself. He has been invited to stay at Brandham in the hope that he will become engaged to Marian.

When Trimingham is first referred to in Chapter 3, mention of his name causes quite a stir; Mr Maudsley makes 'one of his rare contributions to a conversation', and Denys persists in contradicting his mother when she says that Trimingham will miss Goodwood in order to spend the rest of the month at the Hall. Leo learns more about him from Marcus in the following chapter, as the bathing party are walking towards the river. He is told that Trimingham has received severe facial injuries in the South African War, that he is a pleasant person, and that Mrs Maudsley wants Marian to marry him. This last piece of information arouses Leo's jealousy. At this point he believes that Trimingham is of low social status, since no one refers to him as *Mr* Trimingham.

Leo meets Trimingham for the first time one Sunday morning at family prayers. He notices the fearful scar which deforms his face, and immediately feels drawn towards him. This feeling of attraction persists throughout Leo's stay at Brandham Hall, and owes a great deal to Trimingham's attitude to him. Trimingham treats Leo with consideration, letting him down lightly when he realizes the boy has not realized that he is a viscount; and giving him due praise for his successes on the cricket field and at the concert that follows the match. He makes use of Leo as a messenger between Marian and himself, thus providing an ironic counterpoint to the way in which Leo acts as a go-between for Ted and Marian, but he takes care to dignify Leo's status by making sure that he knows that he is to be regarded as the messenger of the gods.

Everything Trimingham does is stylish and bears the mark of a man who is socially at ease because of his privileged position. Everyone defers to him, particularly Mrs Maudsley, and when the Hall party go to church he stays behind to chat to the verger, who acts obsequiously towards him. Trimingham treats everyone courteously, but when Hartley opposes him most dramatically to Ted Burgess it is worth noting how the two characters fare. Ted scores a violent eight-one in his innings for the village, whereas previously Trimingham has batted elegantly, only to be out after having scored a mere eleven runs. Significantly, Leo remarks that, 'A round of applause, subdued and sympathetic and more for him than his play, greeted his return.' As the match nears its climax Trimingham shows great determination to get Ted out, and puts himself on to bowl. His popularity is shown by the generous applause when he takes a wicket, but he only manages to dismiss Ted by means of Leo's brilliant catch.

Trimingham's relationships with Ted and Marian both proceed from a false basis. He tries to persuade Ted to enlist, using his superior social position as a lever, although his motive is patriotic. As he says, '... he's a good chap and I shan't easily find another tenant like him.' He is obviously very much in love with Marian but, as she reveals to Leo, she is unhappy at the thought of marrying him. Here again, it is Trimingham's social status that causes the other character to act as he wishes, and she becomes engaged to him and pays him a lot of attention, though occasionally betraying pique towards him. The depth of Trimingham's feeling for Marian is shown by the fact that he still goes ahead with the marriage arrangements after the scandal over her discovery with Ted.

As Marian says in the Epilogue, 'Hugh was as true as steel. He wouldn't hear a word against me.' This is only what we would expect from his earlier conduct and statements. When he talks to Leo about the death in a duel of his ancestor, the fifth Viscount, he makes it clear that nothing is ever a lady's fault, and he lives up to his own words by his refusal to abandon Marian. In fact, the character of Trimingham encapsulates the best of aristocratic values, while at the same time the character is used by Hartley to indicate the unfairness underlying the fact that some people are able to manipulate others by reason of belonging to a higher social group.

Mrs Maudsley

That tense still look of hers that caught you in its searchlight beam!

Mrs Maudsley is a formidable figure. She is a snob whose main concern is to marry off her daughter to Lord Trimingham. She rules her household with military precision, so much so that when she announces plans for the day's diversions 'it [sounds] like a command'. It is only when she is ill and confined to her room that the others feel they can relax. While she treats Leo quite kindly, she has little feeling for him, as can be seen from her actions on his birthday when she interrogates him in the garden and forces him to go with her to the outhouses in search of Marian. She varies in her attitude towards her children: Marcus is her favourite and shares her secrets; Denys she treats with barely disguised contempt and irritation; while Marian is regarded primarily as a valuable commodity. Mrs Maudsley carried on a battle of wills with Marian throughout the novel, and it is no doubt her anxiety to capture Trimingham for her daughter that causes her to reach the boundaries of hysteria. She is the only member of the family to suspect that Marian is having an affair with someone, and when she receives visible proof that this is the case it unhinges her reason. Marian tells Leo in the Epilogue that it had been necessary for her mother to be locked away in an asylum.

Marcus Maudsley

... a dark-haired, sallow, round-faced boy, with a protruding upper lip that showed his teeth; he was a year younger than I was, and distinguished neither in work nor games, but he managed to get by, as we should say.

Marcus Maudsley is the character nearest in age to Leo, and it is through him that Leo is drawn into the events at Brandham Hall that are to affect him for the rest of his life. He is a year younger than Leo but is much more sophisticated. He is a member of Leo's dormitory at school, and the two boys spend some of their spare time together, but Leo does not consider him to be a special friend. Marcus is not outstanding at games or at schoolwork, but manages to get by. He does not take Leo's side when he is being persecuted by Jenkins and Strode, but is pleased when he appears to vanquish the bullies. Marcus is a snob, and because he is impressed to learn that Leo lives at Court Place, arranges for him to be invited to spend part of the summer at the Maudleys' home in Norfolk.

Hartley uses Marcus in two main ways in the plot. His presence enables Leo and the reader to gain a lot of information about the upper middle class, and he indirectly causes Leo to become involved in Marian's affair with Ted when, because of Marcus's suspected measles, Leo is left so much to his own devices. Finally, Marcus precipitates the violent conclusion of the novel by relaying to Mrs Maudsley the fact that Leo seems to know Marian's real whereabouts when she has claimed to be visiting Nannie Robson but has not in fact been near her.

Leo's reactions to Marcus are mixed. He does not feel very warmly towards him, but usually finds his company a relief after that of the adults at Brandham Hall. However, he does not relish the way in which Marcus tries to get him to agree that the villagers stink at the entertainment in the village hall, and he does not like it when Marcus forces him to have conversations in French in order to put him at a disadvantage. Marcus is shown to be his mother's pet and to share confidences with her. He is a great gossip and is extremely precocious. His lack of discretion amazes Leo when he tells him that Mrs Maudsley is not sure that Marian will stick to her engagement. Linked with Marcus's love of gossip is a sharp tongue, which causes him to speak more harshly about 'the lower orders' than he perhaps feels, and leads him on to taunt Leo about the green bicycle, thus provoking him into revealing the dangerous information that he knows where Marian is.

When Leo returns to school following the catastrophe at Brandham Hall, Marcus and he meet almost as strangers. They are 'polite and distant with each other' and no longer go for walks together. In the Epilogue Leo learns that Marcus was killed in the First World War.

Mr Maudsley

... his personality was so subdued that it seemed to fit in with anything he did.

Mr Maudsley is a leading financier in the City. From Mrs Maudsley's letter to Leo's mother we learn that he has not been very well, but this is not borne out by his appearance or actions in the book. He chooses to play a secondary role in the presence of his wife, yet is obviously a person of determination and organizational ability. In the cricket match, Denys foolishly tries to prevent his father tiring himself, but Mr Maudsley forces him to run, calling out 'Come *on*!' with 'all the authority that [he] so carefully concealed in his daily life'. In the Epilogue, Marian says that her father had great drive, and that he 'took charge and restored order' after the catastrophic events on Leo's birthday in 1900. At Brandham Hall he keeps himself in the background, only seeming to assert himself in room; or when he is called on to play a part in public, as at the entertainment in the village hall after the match, when he makes a witty speech in a characteristically understated way.

Denys Maudsley

He was full of plans and opinions which he would press for more than they were worth – which even I could tell was not very much.

Denys Maudsley is skilfully sketched in by Hartley, but is not given a great deal of individuality. He is a typical young man of his class, with all its prejudices. He lacks any authority, and exists in the novel mainly to illustrate class attitudes and to demonstrate the forcefulness of his mother's personality. When the bathing party approach the river in Chapter 4, Denys is annoyed to find a trespasser swimming there. Upon seeing it is Ted Burgess, he seems 'relieved at not having to make a scene' by trying to order him off; but he shows his snobbery by his comment that Ted 'doesn't swim badly ... for a farmer', and his statement that the Maudsleys 'don't know him socially, of course'.

Whenever Denys is seen with his mother, it is clear she is able to dominate him. Leo notices that she brings out all his clumsiness: '... when he saw her eye on him he always looked as if he was going to drop something – or had dropped it.' Denys has an opinion on everything and likes to give it at length, as he does on the morning of the cricket match. Mrs Maudsley is always merciless towards him, but Leo observes that Mr Maudsley never snubs him, with the exception of the occasion when Denys refuses to take easy runs in the cricket match and seems to be unconscious of his father's growing irritation. In the Epilogue Marian tells Leo that Denys was never quite at home in the family; also that, like Marcus, he was killed in the First World War.

Themes

The major themes that emerge from a reading of *The Go-Between* are: loss of innocence; sexual initiation; Leo's search for a father figure; and class distinction. Before examining Hartley's treatment of these themes it should be emphasized that the novel is not limited to these alone. The book offers many incidental pleasures, such as the descriptions of the cricket match and the concert, both of which can be read on one level as straightforward accounts, 'though at another level they have obvious symbolic and thematic relevance. The student must realize that Hartley is not interested in merely advancing sociological or psychological theories; he is an imaginative novelist writing about certain themes that interest him, but not limiting himself to an examination of those themes by way of a too rigid scheme.

The first two themes, *loss of innocence* and *sexual initiation*, are linked since they both centre on Leo Colston. It is important that Hartley makes Leo a boy who reaches his thirteenth birthday during his stay with the Maudsleys at Brandham Hall. He is just entering puberty, yet still has within himself much of the young child. We learn early in the book that he cannot identify himself with the lion, which is his birth sign, 'because of late I had lost the faculty which, like other children, I had once revelled in, of pretending that I was an animal . . . I was between twelve and thirteen, and I wanted to think of myself as a man' (*Prologue*, p.10). Yet when he reaches Brandham Hall he has to be told by Marcus that Marian is very beautiful before he is able to understand this for himself. Gradually, Leo's feelings for Marian become obvious to the reader and, to some extent, to Leo himself. He wants to serve her and is delighted to be in her company – as when she takes him to Norwich to buy him summer clothes. In spite of feeling let down when he learns from the unopened letter that she and Ted are in love (Chapter 10, p.111), he continues to be attracted to her. He wants to have her to himself, and his attitude towards Ted is ambiguous because he does not really understand that his own feelings of attraction are the first stirrings of sexuality that he has experienced. Some critics have pointed out that the scene where Leo rips apart the deadly nightshade plant in Chapter 21 (pp.240–1) can be read as a sexual encounter between Leo and Marian, who earlier in the novel (Chapter 2, pp.36–8) has been associated so closely in the reader's mind with the plant. This point will be dealt with in more detail in the section on *Symbolism*.

Other references to Leo's reactions to Marian leave us in no doubt that Hartley intends us to be aware of the fact that she stirs him in a sexual way. We know that, for the first time that summer, Leo was delighted by the heat (which had previously been his enemy), and it is hard to avoid the idea that this is connected with his developing sexual awareness, particularly when he says that perhaps Marian *was* the heat (Chapter 22, p.245). In a more overt way Hartley draws the reader's attention to Leo's feelings for Marian in the scene where Marcus describes to Leo how she intends to ride his birthday bicycle into the room 'wearing tights, she says, if Mama will let her, which I doubt. She may have to wear bloomers' (Chapter 19, p.210). Leo has to 'close [his] eyes against the enchanting vision'.

There is much irony underlying the attraction Marian exerts on Leo: throughout the novel he is described as an innocent, yet it is through Marian that he is sexually initiated, in a way that causes him to avoid experience in these matters. When Leo first sees Ted at the river in Chapter 4 he retreats 'almost in fear before that powerful body, which spoke to me of something I did not know' (p.56), and examining Ted's limbs he asks himself, 'What can they do ... to be conscious of themselves?' (p.57). On the visits to Ted's farm Leo's sexual innocence is obvious, in spite of the fact that Ted calls him a big boy for his age, and he begs Ted to tell him the facts about 'spooning'. He is fobbed off until the occasion of his last visit to Ted when he goes to say good-bye to him (Chapter 19). Then Ted says he will keep his promise, and tell him; but Leo loftily refuses (p.216). Ted shows anxiety in case people tell Leo the facts of life in the wrong way, and in retrospect his words contain a terrible irony. Leo's sexual innocence is lost when he sees Marian and Ted – two of the people who mean most to him – in a grotesque embrace on the floor of the outhouse. These two have taken away his innocence in other ways, by making him, as the carrier of their messages, part of an intrigue against the Maudsleys and Lord Trimingham. Now Leo is sexually initiated in a way that is to blight him forever. In this one incident Hartley combines sexual initiation with a loss of innocence. The fact that Leo has been sent to Brandham in such an innocent state is an implicit condemnation of both his education and his upbringing.

Much of the action of *The Go-Between* can be interpreted as *Leo's search for a father figure*. Early in the novel we learn that his father is dead, and that he has only been sent away to school by his mother since his father's death. While his father was alive 'he educated [Leo] himself with the help of a tutor who came out from Salisbury' (Chapter 1, p.23). Leo's father tried to protect him from many things, and we learn that he was against war and was unworldly in his attitudes; in contrast to Leo's mother who 'was always attracted by the things of the world' (Chapter 1, p.23). It soon becomes evident that Leo's mother means a lot to him – probably too much. She influences him greatly and, though he does not entirely agree with her opinions, his temperament makes it difficult for him to cross her.

Mrs Colston is rather an innocent when it comes to the real world, as can be seen by the way she reacts to the news of the injuries to Jenkins and Strode (Chapter 1, p.25), and by an examination of her letter to Leo at Brandham Hall (Chapter 20, pp.218–20). She would like things to be more agreeable than they sometimes are, and is apt to hope that unpleasant things will go away; she leaves Leo unprepared for the pressures he may meet when he is away from her. Perhaps as a result of this, he finds himself looking for a father figure during the weeks he spends in Norfolk: both Ted and Trimingham go some way towards filling this role.

Hartley prepares the reader for Leo's attraction towards these two characters in the Prologue, where the elderly Leo recalls his youthful reactions to the Archer and the Water-carrier in the Zodiac. There are obvious parallels between these figures and Ted and Trimingham. We should note that Hartley forewarns his readers concerning Leo's complicated reactions towards the two men and Marian when he writes, referring to the figures in the Zodiac, 'The two men attracted and repelled me at the same time: perhaps I was jealous of them' (Prologue, p.10).

When we look closely at the actual characters of Ted and Trimingham, as Leo comes into contact with them at Brandham, we find they are both young men in their twenties; but Hartley stresses certain feelings of almost fatherly concern that each exhibits towards Leo – though it should not be overlooked that both men make use of him as a go-between with Marian.

From the first time that Leo sees Ted he is impressed by his physique, and we feel that he would like to possess similar strength. In spite of his very masculine attributes, however, Ted is gentle with Leo when binding up his cut knee; and he looks after him carefully on other occasions when he visits Black Farm. The reader may object that this is only because Ted wants to keep on the right side of Leo, always aware of his importance as a carrier of messages between Marian and himself; but the novel contains sufficient evidence to indicate that Ted feels a genuine warmth towards Leo. Ted's emotion after hearing Leo sing at the concert is real enough, and he appears sincere on the last occasion that the two are seen together, when Leo goes to say good-bye. Hartley has already implied that Ted is a father figure for Leo when he makes him say that telling him about 'spooning' is 'a job for your dad, really' (Chapter 15, p.176). And we should observe the anxiety he now feels that Leo should learn about the facts of life in a positive way (Chapter 19, p.216). In spite of the fact that Ted uses Leo, the reader is left feeling that there is a real bond between them, similar to that experienced in a good father-son relationship.

Leo is also attracted to Trimingham the first time they meet, in spite of the fact that he feels he ought to be prejudiced against him. From Trimingham he learns certain rules of conduct and 'something of the sadness of human life ... its indifference to our wishes' (Chapter 14, p.160). Trimingham has suffered a great deal in the war, and Leo is aware that Marian's actions can make him suffer even more. He is always anxious to please Trimingham, and softens the blow for him when Marian is unkind after he has asked her to sing 'Home,

Sweet Home' at the concert. Trimingham treats Leo with respect and never condescends to him, with the result that he is the person Leo seeks out in the smoking room when he needs to have a phrase in Ted's letter explained (Chapter 18, p.203). The strong impression made by Trimingham on Leo is shown to greatest effect when Leo catches Ted in the cricket match, and Trimingham's 'congratulations were the more precious because they were reserved and understated, they might, in fact, have been addressed to a *man*;' (Chapter 12, p.139). Trimingham is not overtly fatherly to Leo, but his conduct and manner give the boy something to aspire to. Trimingham is ready to treat him as a man, and in this way becomes an object of emulation for the fatherless adolescent boy.

The three themes so far examined have all had to do with Leo. To a certain extent this is also true of the fourth theme – *class distinction* – but Hartley's treatment of the topic permeates the whole novel, involving all his characters, and, by extension, the country itself. What is particularly skilful about Hartley's approach is that he does not feel it necessary to make sweeping statements about the class issue. By limiting the greater part of the action to Brandham Hall and its immediate surroundings, he provides himself with all the ingredients necessary to demonstrate class distinction in action. He has no need to preach, and the book gains in artistry because of this.

Leo belongs to the middle class. His father had been a professional man; his mother is accepted at garden parties in Salisbury; and he himself is sent away to boarding school without too much difficulty, though he realizes that his mother does not have money to throw away. After his success in the affair of Jenkins and Strode, he is drawn into a richer world, that of the Maudsleys. It is important to note that the Maudsleys, though wealthy, carry the marks of social insecurity: they are not sure where they actually stand. Throughout the book their conduct is contrasted with that of the aristocratic Trimingham, to whom everyone automatically defers in spite of the fact he is a member of a dispossessed class – in his case literally, since the Maudsleys are living in the house that had belonged to his family for generations. And it is certain that Marcus and Mrs Maudsley would not have been so ready to invite Leo to stay if they had realized that his address, Court Place, concealed the fact that it was 'quite an ordinary house ... It was not a Court in the grandiloquent sense of the word, such as Maudsley ... believed it to be' (Chapter 1, pp.22–3).

Leo himself is impressed when he arrives at Brandham Hall; he is immediately convinced that its inhabitants are the zodiac figures that so fascinate him. But he has to learn a whole new code of conduct if he is to survive in this world. Peter Bien has pointed out that Leo is a 'social snob', an 'outsider trying to absorb proper manners and outlook', and there is undoubtedly some truth in this view. For example, when Leo is caught by the angry Ted after he falls off the straw stack, he diverts Ted's wrath by letting him know that he is from the Hall, and does not despise him for changing his tune when he learns where Leo comes from (Chapter 7, p.80). In fact, Leo is honest enough to compare Ted's reaction with his own when he alters his attitude towards Trimingham upon realizing he is a Viscount. Nevertheless, Leo sometimes finds it difficult to behave in a manner considered becoming to a member of the ruling class. He usually sees things too clearly for what they are, but he has Marcus there to help him when he shows signs of faltering.

In the words of John Atkins, 'Marcus is a constant fund of information about class behaviour.' He is a tremendous snob in a way that contrasts very much with the natural dignity of Trimingham as well as with Leo's honest feelings. It is Marcus who tells Leo that at night he must drop his clothes on the floor for the servants to pick up, Marcus who tells him that only cads wear made-up ties or would dream of wearing a school cap for a cricket match and, most tellingly, Marcus who tries to make him agree that the 'plebs' at the concert in the village hall stink. He obviously inherits some of these attitudes from his mother who, according to him, didn't want villagers sitting on both sides of her at the supper (Chapter 13, p.151), and it is from Mrs Maudsley's class-ridden attitudes that the whole catastrophe of the novel stems.

The pseudo-democracy represented by the Hall cricket team, in which 'class distinctions melted away and ... the butler, the footman, the coachman, the gardener, and the pantry-boy seemed completely on an equality with us' (Chapter 11, p.127) is not for Mrs Maudsley. Her husband is a successful financier, and she views the affairs of her family from a similar viewpoint. To her Marian is a piece of property to be sold to the highest bidder, not necessarily in terms of money, for Mr Maudsley has enough of that. Mrs Maudsley is angling for Trimingham's title, and when she thinks that Marian has lost her chance of the title because of her affair with Ted her mind becomes unbalanced. She is quite ready to sacrifice her daughter to a marriage without love, even though it involves giving her to a man whose face is frightfully disfigured by the scars of war wounds.

Trimingham is the natural aristocrat, and Hartley endows him with great charm of manner. Nevertheless, there is something unhealthy in the way thát his wishes have to be consulted when he joins the house-party at Brandham Hall; and the scars he carries most probably indicate, in symbolic terms, Hartley's feeling that the aristocracy is flawed, perhaps doomed soon to extinction. This would seem to be borne out by the fact that Trimingham's house has been taken over by members of the merchant class and by the way that, 'Half a century later his grandson is living in a small wing of the house and the rest is let to a girls' school' (John Atkins).

Through the character of Trimingham, Hartley seems to be saying that the old Britain is finished. The Boers have given the first hint that the country is no longer invincible abroad; and Ted's conquest of Marian indicates that members of lower social groups will take over in the future. In the Epilogue, Anne Mulkeen sees hope in 'a healthy merger of the classes'. The eleventh Viscount Trimingham is Ted Burgess's grandson. Miss Mulkeen believes that Hartley is therefore indicating that 'perhaps what was good and beautiful in both Hugh and Ted can blend and carry on in their descendants.' Whether or not this point of view is accurate, few readers will put down *The Go-Between* without feeling that they have been presented with a vivid portrayal of a world in which striking social differences underlie all aspects of everyday living.

Style

In many of the textual notes attention has been drawn to particular features of Hartley's style. In this section the *narrative method and structure* of the novel, and Hartley's use of symbolism, will be examined before going on to consider *other aspects of style.*

Narrative method and structure

The two major points to be noted here are that *The Go-Between* is written in the first person, and that it has what Anne Mulkeen has called a 'double focus', a 'frame-story covering fifty years in this man's life-span, [enabling] us to look back as he does.'

The fact that the novel has a first-person narrator means that almost everything is seen through his eyes. Characters and events reach the reader through the filter of Leo's consciousness, and it is chiefly the consciousness of the Leo of 1900 that we see in action. In addition to Leo's memories of the fateful summer at Brandham Hall, the reader is guided in his own interpretation of events by the responses of the ageing Leo in the Prologue and Epilogue, helped by references to the diary and surviving letters. From time to time in the 1900 narrative Hartley also interpolates interpretative comments by the Leo of 1952.

The framework provided by the Prologue and Epilogue enables us to view the events from a distance along with the narrator. We are aware, as he is, of the ways in which the twentieth century has failed to live up to optimistic expectations, and in these sections in particular we see how life has been soured for Leo by the events of his stay at Brandham Hall so long ago. Any novelist has a primary duty to arouse the interest of his readers in the events of his novel, and it is notable how effectively Hartley builds up our curiosity about the past by means of hints which he drops, particularly in the Prologue and the first two chapters, concerning the far-reaching happenings which are to occur later in the book. The use of this device naturally falls away as the reader is drawn more closely into the story, and is able to see what is happening more clearly than can the innocent Leo of 1900.

As the novel proceeds in its linear development, the comments of the elderly narrator who was presented in the Prologue become less telling until the Epilogue is reached. But the attentive reader will find that authorial intervention is quite frequent throughout the book, so that the narrative of 1900 is never permitted to take place without the sense of the ever-watchful Leo of 1952 observing the action carefully, assessing events and judging motives in a way that parallels the reader's own reaction. There are too many instances to list them all, but the interested reader is directed to the following four examples: 'I have since had the curiosity ... far out' (Chapter 9, p.103); 'At the time I did not wonder ... I know' (Chapter 14, p.154); 'I can see the tea-cups now' (Chapter 15, p.175); 'This is what I think now ... bewildered mind' (Chapter 22, p.246).

The Epilogue enables Hartley to put the events of 1900, and by implication the century, into focus. With Leo the reader sees how Marian has deceived herself about the impact of her love affair with Ted on other people. He is given further evidence of the decline in the influence of the aristocracy when he learns that the eleventh Viscount Trimingham is Ted's grandson, and that he is unable to afford to live in the whole of Brandham Hall. Perhaps more important than either of these things, however, is the fact that the reader sees that Leo learns something positive from his visit to Marian. Sentimental and selfish as she is in the Epilogue, she is able to persuade Leo that 'there's no spell or curse except an unloving heart', and he sets off to the Hall to tell her grandson that he must have no scruples about marrying – that he is not under any curse.

Leo's final entry to the grounds of Brandham Hall and his view of 'the south-west prospect of the Hall, long hidden from my memory' has been seen by Anne Mulkeen as 'a symbol of the attaining of a true vision which has all along been lacking. At last he can see the thing whole.' Whether or not we agree with this symbolic interpretation of the last lines of the novel, there can be no doubt that the Epilogue concludes things in an artistically satisfying way. The story has been told, we have travelled back in time with Leo to see and judge the events that have caused him to become what he is now, and the Epilogue serves to draw all the strands together, thus enabling us to make our final decision as to the accuracy and relevance of what we have seen.

In addition to those already mentioned, Hartley makes use, in *The Go-Between*, of perhaps less obvious structural devices. In the textual notes attention is frequently directed to instances where Hartley points forward to important future happenings in the novel, or reminds his readers of something that has occurred earlier. His use of symbolism can also be seen to play a part structurally, as well as fulfilling other purposes. Finally, it may be helpful to examine two other features used by Hartley in ways that contribute to the novel's structure: two spells cast by the Leo of 1900; and the letters and messages that are such a central feature of *The Go-Between*.

The major framework of the novel's Prologue and Epilogue has a parallel in Leo's spell against Jenkins and Strode (Prologue, p.14), and the one he invokes to break the spell he believes Ted has cast on Marian (Chapter 21, pp.231–40). Structurally the two spells are placed effectively in the book, one very near the beginning and one near the end. Each spell carries a great deal of emotional weight, which is reinforced by the language used to record it and by the emphasis on the dramatic circumstances in which it takes place. Although it is obvious that Leo cannot really control events in a supernatural fashion, things do fall out in such a way as to bring about the aims for which the spells have been formulated. Unfortunately, in each case the result is too drastic. In the former instance Leo's two tormentors are nearly killed in a fall from the roof, while the affair between Ted and Marian is stopped, but at the expense of Ted's life, Mrs Maudsley's sanity, and Leo's future emotional development.

Letters and messages play an important part in the structure of *The Go-Between*, their placing resembling beads loosely strung along the thread of the plot. Every reader will recall the way in which the three major adult characters, Ted, Marian and Trimingham, make use of Leo as their go-between. Trimingham calls him Mercury, and he delights in seeing himself as the messenger of the gods of Brandham. The messages he takes for Trimingham are of a harmless nature, informing Marian that she has left her hymn book behind, asking her to play croquet, or to sing a special song at the cricket supper. The letters and messages which Leo takes between Ted and Marian are of a different character. From the outset they involve deceit, as Leo is told that they are business communications which must be kept secret at all costs. Ultimately they lead to events causing death, shame and emotional sterility.

The reader should note, however, the ways in which Hartley uses other letters in the book. For example, Leo is drawn into the world of Brandham Hall by Mrs Maudsley's letter to his mother, asking her to let him spend most of July in Norfolk (Chapter 1, p.29). In addition to starting the main plot of the novel and informing the reader about the social position of the Maudsleys, this letter contains information about Mrs Maudsley's health, thus preparing us for later events. Other important letters in the book are those in which Leo writes to his mother twice in one day, first asking her to allow him to stay longer (Chapter 14, p.156) and later, having been made unhappy by Marian's accusation that he is a Shylock, begging her to send a telegram calling him home (Chapter 16, pp.178–9). This second letter is crucial to the outcome of the novel. For several days Leo passes the time convinced that his mother will do what he asks, only to receive an uncomprehending letter from her in which she tells him that it will be better for him to stay at Brandham Hall, as 'All this will be an *experience* for you, my darling' (Chapter 20, p.220). Disappointed, Leo does as he is told and is forced to witness the discovery of Ted and Marian in the outhouse on the very afternoon that Mrs Maudsley has seen Marian stuff into his pocket a letter for Ted, which she claims is intended for Nannie Robson.

Hartley makes great dramatic use of this last letter. In the Epilogue the elderly Leo comes upon it among his papers, 'sealed down but unaddressed'. When he reads it he discovers that Marian wanted to revert to the usual time for meeting Ted – Leo, it will be remembered, had told her a different time, in the hope of breaking her attachment to Ted – and that the bicycle had been intended as an aid to speedy delivery of the lovers' messages. Reading this last letter causes Leo to shed tears for the first time since leaving Brandham Hall in 1900 (Epilogue, p.268).

The final messages used by Hartley in the novel are to be found in those pages dealing with the elderly Leo's return to Brandham. He asks the eleventh Viscount Trimingham to convey a message to Marian saying that he would like to see her and, after their talk, finds himself reverting to the role of messenger for her when he returns to Brandham Hall charged with the duty of explaining to Ted's grandson that Marian's love for Ted was nothing to be ashamed of. Leo contemplates ignoring Marian's last message – 'And why should I go on this preposterous errand? I hadn't promised to and I wasn't a child, to be ordered about' (p.280). Nevertheless, though no longer a child under the influence of adults with power over him, he once again becomes 'the go-between'.

Symbolism

In his *Dictionary of Literary Terms* (1963), J. R. Harmsworth defines symbolism as 'the use of one object to represent or suggest another'. *The Go-Between* depends for a great deal of its effectiveness upon the reader's reactions to Hartley's use of symbolism. At the outset it should be noted that this symbolism is of two kinds: that which is apparent to the Leo of 1900; and that of which he is unconscious, but which will be observed by the attentive reader.

From a reading of the Prologue it becomes evident that the young Leo likes to view things symbolically. When he is given a diary for the year 1900 by his mother it is more than a diary to him. He is full of the sense that the year 1900 is the first year of the century, and the idea holds 'an almost mystical appeal' for him. He believes that the coming century will be 'the realization, on the part of the whole world, of the hopes that [he entertains] for himself' (Prologue, p.10). The date on the diary is surrounded by the signs of the zodiac, which Leo invests with magic and power in his imagination. He is attracted towards the two male figures of the Archer and the Water-carrier, but his chief object of devotion is the figure of the Virgin.

When Leo arrives at Brandham Hall he becomes aware of the fact that his private fantasy concerning the figures of the zodiac is applicable to the people he meets there. Trimingham calls him Mercury, the messenger of the gods, and he pictures 'himself threading his way through the Zodiac, calling on one star after another' (Chapter 8, p.91). He identifies Marian with the Virgin, while the other figures at Brandham become 'the companions of the Zodiac' (Chapter 7, p.77). However, as the novel proceeds, the ironic implications of some aspects of Leo's symbolic fantasy become apparent to the reader.

Before considering Hartley's symbolism in relation to particular characters, it may be helpful to look at some examples of his use of symbolism in relation to the broad themes of the novel. Two symbols stand out above all: those of the Boer War and the weather. Throughout the book Hartley ensures that his readers are kept aware of the fact that his seemingly peaceful story is taking place against a background of the war in South Africa. The book contains many references to actual events of the war, but Hartley uses it chiefly in a symbolic way in relation to the respective positions of Ted and Lord Trimingham, and with regard to the social changes that were shortly to take place in Britain. Unknown to Trimingham, he and Ted are rivals for Marian. The Boers were the underdogs in the wars in South Africa, but ultimately won their battle to direct their own affairs when the Transvaal and the Orange Free State received self-government in 1907. Bearing this in mind, it is significant that Trimingham has returned, hideously scarred, from South Africa; and that the villagers in the cricket match are likened by Leo to Boers 'who did not have much in the way of equipment by our standards, but could give a good account of themselves, none the less' (Chapter 11, p.127).

Ted is the hero of the village's innings, with the implication that he and his kind will ultimately triumph over the Triminghams of the world. He does so, of course, as it is his child who inherits the Trimingham title, but just to show that Hartley avoids being too schematic in his use of symbolism, it should be remembered that Trimingham dismisses Ted in the cricket match by means of Leo's catch.

Finally, in connection with the symbolism of the Boers it should be noted that Leo sees the cricket match in terms of war when he hears 'men's voices calling each other in tones of authority and urgency, as if life had suddenly become more serious, as if a battle were in prospect' (Chapter 11, p.126), and in Chapter 12 he sees the symbolic overthrow of the representatives of the Hall when Ted hits a mighty six: 'A scatter of small boys darted off to look for it and while they were hunting the fieldsmen lay down on the grass; only Ted and his partner and the two umpires remaining standing, looking like victors on a stricken field' (p. 134).

As previously mentioned, Hartley is merely making use of recorded fact when he sets *The Go-Between* in the stiflingly hot summer of 1900. But he makes good symbolic use of the background of heat, first in relation to Leo's developing sexual awareness, and also in connection with the build-up of events at Brandham Hall towards their violent conclusion in the outhouse. Prior to the summer of 1900, Leo had considered the heat to be an enemy, and it continues to be one until Marian takes him to Norwich to buy him summer clothes. From then on he associates himself with the heat, visiting the game-larder to check the thermometer, hoping always that it will reach record heights. Accompanying the bathing party (Chapter 4), Leo longs to experience 'complete, corporeal union with the summer' (p.50), and the links with his sexual development are stressed. From this point onwards, Leo's fascination with the heat is emphasized, and the implication is that this is strongly connected with his love for Marian.

The observant reader will notice the way in which the weather in the novel is used by Hartley to create mood. As the shattering conclusion approaches, the weather changes. It is still hot, but on the Saturday of the cricket match (the first occasion on which the forces of anarchy are seen to triumph over aristocratic values), 'the thermometer only rose to seventy-eight, clouds came up – the first clouds I had seen at Brandham since I came – and the sun shone fitfully' (Chapter 11, p.120). As the match proceeds, Leo is aware of an enormous cloud, which has obvious symbolic significance (Chapter 12, pp.133–4). The days draw on until, on the morning of Leo's birthday, he wakes up to find that rain is threatening (Chapter 22, p.242); and the projected excursion to Beeston Castle in the afternoon is abandoned because of the weather. Most significantly, his interrogation by Mrs Maudsley is only brought to an end by rumblings of thunder, followed instantly by rain (Chapter 23, p.256); and the lamps have to be lit at his birthday tea because of the darkness outside. The final dreadful scenes are played out against the background of the storm. Marian fails to appear at the party, and when the carriage returns without her from Nannie Robson's Leo is forced to accompany Mrs Maudsley to the outhouses through the downpour. The discovery of Ted and Marian takes place against the sound of rain pattering on the battered roofs of the huts.

Hartley's use of symbolism in connection with the main characters of the novel is very effective and some instances have been pointed out in the textual notes, but it may be useful at this point to examine certain symbols that are linked with Marian, Ted and Leo.

The most striking symbol in the book is that of the Deadly Nightshade plant. It is important to note that, when it is first described in Chapter 2, it is closely linked with a description of Marian. Marcus has told Leo that she is very beautiful, and in the space of two and a half pages (pp.36–8) Hartley presents his readers with the essence of the novel in symbolic terms. The Deadly Nightshade is evil yet beautiful, and while Marian's beauty in repose is evident, her face 'wore a stern brooding look that her small curved nose made almost hawk-like. She looked formidable then . . .' (p.37). Leo decides not to tell Mrs Maudsley about the presence of the poisonous plant in the outhouse since he cannot bear the idea of its 'lusty limbs withering on a rubbish heap or crackling in a fire: all that beauty being destroyed' (p.38). The language used here connects the plant with Marian and with Leo's unconscious desire to possess her.

The point is further emphasized in later descriptions in Chapter 17 (pp.191–2) and in Chapter 21 (p.240). One critic has likened the latter description of the Deadly Nightshade to that of a harlot standing in a doorway beckoning Leo inside, and there can be no doubting the erotic force of the passage. Significantly, although Leo succeeds in destroying the plant, he is showered with grains of earth as he uproots it, implying perhaps that though he has tried to cast out sexuality he is going to be badly affected in the future by his involvement with Marian.

Ted Burgess is linked with symbols of life and death. He is

first seen bathing in Chapter 4. Water is a life-giving element, and from then onwards Ted's links with nature are stressed. Hartley makes a great deal of his physicality. For example, Leo sees how ill at ease he appears in a lounge suit and starched collar in the village hall: 'The more clothes he put on, the less he looked himself' (Chapter 13, p.142); and when Leo visits Black Farm in Chapter 15 he finds Ted stripped to the waist in his kitchen. Here Hartley combines life and death imagery, since Ted is in the act of cleaning his gun. The gun has very obvious phallic connotations, but the author is at the same time pointing forward to the time when Ted will return to his kitchen to blow his brains out after being discovered with Marian. Even earlier in the novel, Hartley has fore-warned the reader of the outcome of the affair between Ted and Marian, when Leo takes a letter to Ted and finds him standing with his gun, waiting for rabbits to emerge from shelter as the reaper gathers in the last of the standing corn. Death and life exist side by side, symbolized by the gun and the harvest. As Ted takes the letter from Leo he smears it with blood, presaging an unhappy outcome to the affair with Marian; and it is hard to believe that Hartley did not wish his readers to think of 'the grim reaper' (Death) when he makes Leo have 'the fancy that he was a sheaf the reaper had forgotten and that it would come back for him' (Chapter 9, p.101).

Leo is symbolically connected with Ted in other ways: in particular when he defeats him by catching him in the cricket match; and when he eclipses him at the concert. Leo is very aware of the fact that he has overcome Ted on both occasions, but does not realize that he is indirectly to be the cause of Ted's death, when Mrs Maudsley – alerted by Marcus to the fact that Leo knows where Marian really is when she says she is visiting Nannie Robson – takes Leo to the outhouses.

But perhaps the most obvious symbol used in connection with Leo is his green suit. As soon as he puts it on it gives him the freedom to become a different person: he recognizes that it releases the real Leo. Even though he is deeply hurt by Marcus's revelation that Marian chose the suit because green is the appropriate colour for him – signifying that he is in-experienced and gullible – he recognizes that the green suit frees his imagination to go roving as Robin Hood in the greenwood with his Maid Marian. There is hideous irony in the fact that it is Marian's conduct that is to blight life for Leo for over fifty years, causing him to put on one side the world of the imagination and take up the study of facts.

Other aspects of style

One could write at great length about other distinctive features of the style of *The Go-Between*, but discussion here will be confined to a consideration of: 1, the variety of the language in the novel; 2, the quality of the dialogue; 3, Hartley's use of repetitive constructions in his sentences; and 4, his careful attention to punctuation. It should, however, be emphasized that the student must feel free to comment on other aspects of the book's style, as they strike him. The important thing is for him to be able to support his views by direct reference to the text if he is faced with a question on style in an examination. It need hardly be added that the general reader will find he will gain a great deal of pleasure if he trains himself to look at this or any novel with a view to discovering not only what the author is saying but the means he is using to say it. Indeed, it can be argued that the two are indivisible.

1 *The Go-Between* is notable for the *variety of language* it contains. To begin with, it is narrated by a member of the comfortably off middle class, and chiefly deals with events which have taken place over fifty years before. The background of privilege against which the action is played out requires a fairly leisured manner of telling the story. Accordingly, the novel builds up slowly to its climax in Chapter 23, having reached a lesser climax in the central sections concerning the cricket match and the concert. Hartley's vocabulary is that of an educated member of the middle class, and even when events take a violent turn his method of describing them does not require him to descend to violent language. The tone is cool and controlled even when the incidents concerned are passionate and overpowering. As we have seen in the section on *Symbolism*, the reason for this lies partly in the oblique manner in which Hartley chooses to obtain his effects. By so doing he does not lessen their impact; and when violence does break out (as in the case of Mrs Maudsley's screams when she finds Ted and Marian together) the contrast is remarkable.

We would expect the language of the elderly Leo to be restrained, but it is interesting to see the various types of language associated with his younger self. Early in the novel we learn that he wants the entries in his diary to 'reach a high standard of literary attainment', and it is his pretentious use of the word 'vanquished' that leads to the 'spell' that seems to cause the downfall of his enemies, Jenkins and Strode. When Leo reaches Brandham Hall, we are given examples of other types of language he has at his command. He is able to talk a kind of demotic French with Marcus, and the schoolboy slang and insults the pair exchange serve to bring home to the reader how young Leo really is, thus emphasizing the pathos of his situation when he is caught up in a world of adult intrigue, which he is unable fully to understand. Leo finds that he is able to converse with adults such as Trimingham and Ted, but his childish incomprehension is frequently referred to in the novel.

The reader learns from Leo's narrative that he is under great pressure at Brandham Hall, but Hartley skilfully inserts into the book two examples of Leo's writing that vividly demonstrate that pressure to the reader. The first is the letter he writes to his mother asking her to call him back home (Chapter 16, pp.178–9), in which the spelling mistakes betray his agitation, and the second is the extract from his diary describing the spell to be made with the Deadly Nightshade plant (Chapter 21, pp.238–9). There are comments in the textual notes on the way that Hartley here uses the language of the laboratory. The irony is that chemistry experiments are carried out under controlled conditions: as Leo discovers, life cannot be so easily managed.

The student should also notice Hartley's extremely beautiful descriptive passages. We have already examined the account of the Deadly Nightshade in the section on *Symbolism*, but it repays scrutiny as a straightforward description of the plant. Other passages that the student is recommended to examine are: the beginning of Chapter 12 (pp.133–4), where Leo looks at his surroundings before Ted Burgess goes in to bat; and the description of the birthday party in which everything singled out by Hartley adds to the tension Leo is feeling (Chapter 23, pp.257–60).

2 *The quality of the dialogue* in the novel can be demonstrated on almost any page, but the reader should look closely at two sections involving Mrs Maudsley. Both occur towards the end of the book. In Chapter 22 (pp.249–50) the unfortunate Denys is unwise enough to draw his mother's attention to the fact that she has engineered Leo into doing what *she* wants on his birthday. In the space of twenty lines Mrs Maudsley demolishes his arguments in a way that allows of no opposition. The icy reasonableness of her tone is well conveyed by her words alone, without the necessity for Hartley's three interpolated lines describing Mrs Maudsley's actions in the course of the exchange. The other example is to be found in the following chapter when Mrs Maudsley has seen Marian slip a note into Leo's pocket. She takes Leo off to see the gardens; and the whole section is packed with tension as Mrs Maudsley waits to pounce on any mistake he makes. Pages 254–6 will repay very close examination, if the student bears in mind Hartley's ability to link the overall symbolism of the novel with the realistic dialogue, which reflects the strength and ruthlessness of Mrs Maudsley.

3 One of the characteristic features of Hartley's style is his habit of using *repetitive constructions in his sentences*. He is fond of a build-up of nouns for rhetorical effect, as in 'The decorations, the colours, the heat, the almost overpowering sense of matiness' (Chapter 13, p.141); and the reader soon becomes aware of his fondness for using other parts of speech in clusters of three. Examples are 'soundless, featureless, and motionless' (Chapter 14, p.153); the triple use of 'jealous' (Chapter 14, p.154); and 'but now it was gloomy and forbidding and rather frightening' (Chapter 17, p.186).

On other occasions Hartley shows a predilection for triple structures within his sentences: for example, in Chapter 21 (p.234) with the repetition of 'like' in the sentence beginning 'There would have been no ridicule'. And at one point in the novel he uses triple repetition outside the bounds of one particular sentence to achieve a very poignant effect: this is in Chapter 19 (pp.215–16), when Leo tells Ted three times that he has not told anyone about the meetings between him and Marian.

The student will find many more examples of Hartley's liking for repetitive constructions and must make up his own mind as to whether the device is used too frequently. The final example is a paragraph from Chapter 20 (p.228), in which the impression of Leo's adoration of Marian is reinforced by the inclusion of her name nine times in three sentences. The writer has taken a great risk here, but it is successful.

4 It might be argued that the best punctuation passes the reader by, and that an author should ensure that his own punctuation is not obtrusive, but at certain points in *The Go-Between* Hartley owes his effects to his *careful attention to punctuation*. In particular his use of the colon and semi-colon should be noted. Examples of skilful use of the colon can be found in Chapter 12 (p.134) in two consecutive sentences describing Leo's reactions to Ted at the wicket. In the sentence beginning, 'I was puzzled', Leo's factual summing up of his wishes about the cricket until this moment is placed after the colon in the manner of the answer to a sum. The colon in the second sentence, which begins 'The first ball', serves a more dramatic function. Here again the second half of the sentence contains a kind of response to an implied question in the first half, and the unexpectedness of that response is emphasized by the heavy pause the colon represents.

Hartley's use of the semi-colon is equally effective. In Chapter 11 (p.130) Leo is describing Mr Maudsley batting. The second part of the sentence beginning 'He had no style' elaborates on the flat statement made before the semi-colon. Much the same effect is achieved in the other two examples, which are to be found in consecutive sentences in Chapter 13 (p.149). The second part of the sentence beginning 'That was just it' expands on the reason why no one will come forward with a secular song, and refers back to the last sentence of the previous paragraph; while the semi-colon in the sentence beginning, 'It was getting late' causes the reader to pause momentarily before proceeding, in the second half of the sentence, to gather further information about Leo's mood.

General questions and sample answer in note form

1 *The Go-Between* has been called 'a study of innocence suddenly overwhelmed by experience'. Do you agree with this description?

2 A critic has written that *The Go-Between* 'is concerned above all with sin, evil, and even horror'. How far is this an accurate assessment?

3 Consider the effectiveness of Hartley's use of symbolism in *The Go-Between*. Refer closely to the text in your answer.

4 Compare and contrast the characters of Lord Trimingham and Ted Burgess, and examine the part played by each in the novel.

5 L. P. Hartley once said, 'The truth is that I can see more easily through the eyes of a child than through those of an adult.' How successfully does he convey, in *The Go-Between*, the impression of events seen through the eyes of a child?

6 Discuss the importance in the novel of the descriptions of the cricket match and the entertainment in the village hall.

7 Write a character study of Marian, paying close attention to two scenes in which you consider that she is most vividly portrayed.

8 Discuss the importance of the backgrounds and settings in *The Go-Between*.

9 Which two episodes in the novel do you find most dramatic, and why?

10 Write an essay on the importance of letters and messages in *The Go-Between*.

11 Examine Hartley's presentation of Leo's relationship with *either* Ted Burgess *or* Lord Trimingham.

12 How effective is *The Go-Between* as an evocation of the life of the leisured classes at the beginning of the twentieth century?

13 What aspects of Hartley's style in this novel have impressed you most? Illustrate your answer by close reference to the text.

14 Show the significance of the Prologue and the Epilogue in relation to the novel as a whole.

15 Outline the reasons you would give for reading *The Go-Between*, if you were recommending the novel to someone who knew nothing about it.

16 Compare Marian with any other major female character in one of your other books.

17 How does Hartley's presentation of childhood in *The Go-Between* differ from that of any other author whose work you have studied?

18 Indicate how you would set about dramatizing an important scene for one of your chosen books.

19 Compare any two novels you have read recently in which the story is told in the first person.

20 Write an extract from the imaginary diary of a major character in one of the books you have been studying which clarifies his or her actions for the reader.

Suggested notes for essay answer to question 1

(a) Define 'innocence' – state of being sinless/unacquainted with evil; the 'experience' – knowledge gained as a result of observation or awareness of facts and events.

(b) These terms chiefly relevant to Leo: at school aware of evil when attacked by bullies. Nevertheless sexually ignorant although he is between twelve and thirteen years old and wishes to think of himself as a man.

At Brandham: Leo shown as still a child. Believes
(i) Marian beautiful because Marcus says so and
(ii) Deadly Nightshade beautiful because mother's botany book says so. Leo is shown as sometimes out of depth socially (initially unaware that Trimingham is a lord). After trip to Norwich 'forgets' the hour spent away from Marian in Cathedral. Unaware of the significance of Marian's meeting with man (realized by adult Leo in Epilogue to have been Ted).

(c) Tries to get Ted to tell him about 'spooning'. Dimly aware of male/female attraction.

(d) First loss of innocence when he realizes that the messages carried between Ted and Marian were love letters. When walking with Marcus leads him away from outhouses, having recognized Ted's voice.

(e) Fails to understand references to Ted's sexual reputation in Chapter 18.

(f) Learns about importance of social class in male/female relationships when Marian bursts into tears in Chapter 20.

(g) Leo has been compromised by being made to lie to Mrs Maudsley to protect Marian.

(h) Leo's sexual innocence suddenly demolished when forced by Mrs Maudsley to go into hut where they come upon Marian and Ted making love.

(i) *Conclusion*: Leo's loss of innocence destroyed his life for next fifty years. Blames himself for betrayal of everyone at Brandham: fails to see that adults had exploited him. Visit to Marian in Epilogue helps to redeem Leo. Realizes that he has a stronger grasp of reality than Marian, who has deceived herself for years, yet is moved by her insistence that 'there's no spell or curse except an unloving heart', even though he claims to be a 'foreigner in the world of the emotions'. Finally, agree with overall truth of description in the question.

Further reading

Some lively criticism of Hartley has been published in recent years, but the student's first aim should be to read more of his fiction, particularly the novels. Another book dealing with childhood and set in the Norfolk which Hartley knew so well is *The Shrimp and the Anemone* (1944). A rewarding comparison can be made between the central character of Eustace in this novel and Leo in *The Go-Between*. The student who is interested in the problems of moral responsibility which concern both characters is advised to read a later novel, *The Brickfield* (1964), in which Hartley returns to some of the same questions.

Short articles and sections on Hartley can be found in many books on the modern English novel, but the reader looking for lengthy discussion of his work is recommended to read the following:

John Atkins, *Six Novelists Look at Society* (John Calder) (A survey of the work of six twentieth-century writers which includes a 35-page chapter on Hartley)

Peter Bien, *L. P. Hartley* (Chatto and Windus)

Paul Bloomfield, *L. P. Hartley* (Longman Group, revised edition, 1970)

(A booklet devoted entirely to Hartley, no. 217 of the 'Writers and their Work' series.)

Edward T. Jones, *L. P. Hartley* ('Twayne's English Authors' series.)

Anne Mulkeen, *Wild Thyme, Winter Lightning: The Symbolic Novels of L. P. Hartley* (Hamish Hamilton)

The advanced student may be interested in reading *The Novelist's Responsibility*, a collection of L. P. Hartley's literary essays and lectures, published in 1967 by Hamish Hamilton.

Finally, any reader who wishes to examine literary influences and parallels is recommended to read Henry James's novel, *What Maisie Knew*. Many aspects of the theme of this book and the technical problems which faces James in writing it have obvious relevance to a detailed study of *The Go-Between*.